Cambridge Elements

Elements in the Philosophy of Ludwig Wittgenstein
edited by
David G. Stern
University of Iowa

AF292345

WITTGENSTEIN ON COLOUR, 1916–1950

Andrew Lugg
University of Ottawa

CAMBRIDGE
UNIVERSITY PRESS

Shaftesbury Road, Cambridge CB2 8EA, United Kingdom

One Liberty Plaza, 20th Floor, New York, NY 10006, USA

477 Williamstown Road, Port Melbourne, VIC 3207, Australia

314–321, 3rd Floor, Plot 3, Splendor Forum, Jasola District Centre,
New Delhi – 110025, India

103 Penang Road, #05–06/07, Visioncrest Commercial, Singapore 238467

Cambridge University Press is part of Cambridge University Press & Assessment,
a department of the University of Cambridge.

We share the University's mission to contribute to society through the pursuit
of education, learning and research at the highest international levels of excellence.

www.cambridge.org
Information on this title: www.cambridge.org/9781009565967
DOI: 10.1017/9781009566001

When citing this work, please include a reference to the DOI 10.1017/9781009566001

First published 2025

A catalogue record for this publication is available from the British Library

ISBN 978-1-009-56596-7 Hardback
ISBN 978-1-009-56599-8 Paperback
ISSN 2632-7112 (online)
ISSN 2632-7104 (print)

Wittgenstein on Colour, 1916–1950

Elements in the Philosophy of Ludwig Wittgenstein

DOI: 10.1017/9781009566001
First published online: February 2025

Andrew Lugg
University of Ottawa

Author for correspondence: Andrew Lugg, andrewlugg@sympatico.ca

Abstract: A study of Wittgenstein on the logic of colour concepts. His remarks on the subject in the *Tractatus* are considered first, then the remarks he drafted when he returned to philosophy after a decade away from it, then his treatment of colour concepts during the next two decades followed by the remarks in *Remarks on Colour*. The emphasis is on the problems he examines and the solutions he proposes. His discussion of colour incompatibility is defended, his examination of colour concepts in the 1930s and 1940s detailed and explained, and the remarks he composed at the end of his life considered with an eye to why they were written and what they add to remarks previously composed. It is argued that his aims are different from those normally attributed to him and, while he achieves a great deal, he does not resolve all the problems he tackles.

Keywords: Wittgenstein, colour, 1916–1950, philosophy, commentary

ISBNs: 9781009565967 (HB), 9781009565998 (PB), 9781009566001 (OC)
ISSNs: 2632-7112 (online), 2632-7104 (print)

Contents

Introduction

In this Element I attempt to provide a comprehensive and thorough summary of Wittgenstein's remarks on the logic of colour concepts. While his comments on ethics, aesthetics, religion and other subjects he says little about have been much discussed, his treatment of colour concepts has been little studied, his discussion of the impossibility of the joint occurrence of two colours aside. It is generally overlooked that in addition to referring to colour regularly to illustrate this or that philosophical point, he has much on the logic of colour concepts. He found the special nature of such concepts intriguing and devoted much effort, early and late, to clarifying them and to grappling with logical problems that arise when they are subjected to critical scrutiny. No question that he had more to say about language, meaning, logic, mathematics and psychological concepts than about what he referred to as 'the problem of colour' but getting straight about our use of colour language was for him no minor business and as long as he did not have the matter fully under control he continued to work at it. How he handled the topic also illuminates in no small way the kind of philosopher he was, his way of tackling philosophical problems and what he believed philosophy can and cannot be expected to do.

I cover Wittgenstein's writings on the logic of colour concepts from the time he began serious work in philosophy to the last year or so of his life. Section 1 is devoted to remarks drafted in 1916–1918, remarks that treat colour in a novel way, a way never subsequently criticized, only amended and supplemented. Next, in Section 2, I consider how Wittgenstein handled the topic when he returned to philosophy in 1929 after the better part of a decade away from it. Then, in Sections 3 and 4, I discuss the observations about colour concepts he composed in the 1930s, a period commonly dubbed transitional, and the 1940s, years in which he is widely reckoned to have had next to nothing to say on the topic. The burden of these sections is that there is more about colour concepts, and more that is important, than ordinarily supposed. Finally, in Sections 5 and 6, I examine Wittgenstein's treatment of colour concepts in manuscripts composed in 1950, notably the remarks in *Remarks on Colour*, a posthumously published compilation of his last thoughts on the subject. (Sections 5 and 6 complement the detailed discussion of *Remarks on Colour* in my *Wittgenstein's Remarks on Colour*.) At the end of each section I mention other discussions of the material, in particular those that treat the material differently from how I do.

Wittgenstein was chiefly interested in meaning, sense and significance, and when discussing colour, he devotes the lion's share of his attention to ways in which colour language is used in everyday life (and by extension in science and elsewhere). Not without reason, he accepted that language is our chief, if not our sole, means of thinking and talking about colour (or anything else), and he zeroes in on how colour is thought and talked about. He does not, as sometimes supposed, take us to be imprisoned in language but holds that language is used to describe, explain, communicate about a world separate from language (aside from when language is itself under the microscope). Moreover he confines himself pretty much to a consideration of linguistic necessities and possibilities. For him only a priori features of colour language (and correlatively the necessities and possibilities embedded in it) are grist for the philosopher's mill, a posteriori fact being the exclusive province of science. He does not refrain from mentioning scientific results about colour but considers them no more significant for philosophical investigation than made-up results. At the heart of his discussion is an interest in what he variously calls the logic of colour concepts and the grammar of colour language.

I am at pains to do justice to Wittgenstein's antipathy to philosophy as it is usually done. However hard his philosophical approach is to pin down, it was clearly very much his own, and I have attempted to keep in mind that he once said: 'Work in philosophy is actually closer to working on oneself. On one's own understanding. On the way one sees things. (And what one demands of them)' (BT: 407; also CV: 24). There are plenty of passages concerning colour that can be regimented as arguments with premises and conclusions but only at the expense of missing what Wittgenstein intends to convey. To appreciate his philosophical message, it is essential to follow in his footsteps and allow him to speak for himself. As I see it, one obtains a feel for his characteristic style only when one takes him at his word and resists the temptation to attribute to him philosophical theses or doctrines. I do not belabour the point but should like to think I show that he pioneers a distinctive way of philosophizing and means to change how 'one sees things' rather than tender philosophical results.

Along the way I defend various conclusions. First, I maintain that there is a lot to be said for Wittgenstein's treatment of colour concepts in the *Tractatus* and he is wrongly upbraided for failing to explain the impossibility of two colours, red and green for instance, occurring together. Secondly, I argue that Wittgenstein's changing views about colour incompatibility were not responsible for his developing a new approach to philosophy but rather the other way around, his changing views about other philosophical matters prompting him to change his views about colour incompatibility. Thirdly, in opposition to the assumption that his late thought could not be more different from his early thought, I contend that post-1929/1930 he does not repudiate the idea of a 'logic of colour concepts' advanced in the *Tractatus* but rather promotes a more sophisticated view of what it involves. Fourthly, I claim that Wittgenstein's final discussion of colour is similarly of a piece with his earlier discussion and challenge the contention that after 1945 he shifted his basic philosophical stance as opposed to developing it further (at least as regards the logic of colour). Fifthly, I question the usual view of why and when *Remarks on Colour* was written and urge that Wittgenstein returned to the topic because he had no account of the logical impossibility of transparent white. My main hope, however, is that it will be granted that Wittgenstein's remarks on colour should not be left to languish in the limbo to which they are nearly always consigned.

As there is more than enough for a short book about colour in Wittgenstein's published remarks, I refrain from quoting from his *Nachlass* and reports of lectures, except when helpful or unavoidable. I do not pretend to mention everything that Wittgenstein says about colour down to the last comment but attempt to indicate the main lines of his thought and explain how his later writings echo or diverge from earlier ones. I use the translation of the *Tractatus* supervised by C.K. Ogden, this having been vetted by Wittgenstein, and I rely on published translations of other works apart from very occasionally making small changes in the interests of accuracy and clarity. I also follow the practice of referring to Wittgenstein's remarks by section or page number supplemented by an indication of the source and date of the composition of the material when instructive and known. (Short references to Wittgenstein's and other philosophers' works are provided in the text with full details in the bibliography at the end of the Element.) To keep things simple, I abjure polemical references to the secondary literature, avoid cluttering the text with footnotes, eschew italics except in quotations, and add or drop capital letters at the beginning of quotations when the context calls for it and there is no resulting confusion.

1 Wittgenstein on Colour, 1916–1918

'Colours seem to present us with a riddle'

Perhaps reflecting on his own case, Wittgenstein observed in 1948 that 'colours are a stimulus to philosophizing' (CV: 76). Certainly they fascinated him and spurred him to put pen to paper. For him, as he added (with a play on words of a sort he was fond of): 'Colours seem to present us with a riddle, a riddle that stimulates us – not one that exasperates us [*das uns anregt – nicht aufregt*]'. He had no quarrel with well-established empirical facts and theories about colour and would, for instance, have known and accepted without argument that coloured pigments combine 'subtractively', coloured lights 'additively' (so that combining red and green lights results in a yellow light whereas combining blue and yellow pigments results in green pigment). Nor would he have needed to be told that some colours are perceived as cool, others as warm (compare blue with red), that some colours are aesthetically pleasing, some not, some combinations harmonious, others discordant. He never questioned such facts, just regarded them as lacking philosophical interest. His view, as uncontroversial as it is widespread, was that empirical truth falls under the jurisdiction of the appropriate science or related branch of learning. It is not for nothing that he wrote in 1949: 'Scientific questions may interest me, but they never really grip me. Only *conceptual & aesthetic* questions have that effect on me. At bottom it leaves me cold whether scientific problems are solved; but not those other questions' (CV: 91).

It is central to Wittgenstein's conception of philosophy, not just his discussion of colour, that philosophical investigation is different from scientific investigation and that conflating them causes no end of trouble. He was not anti-science, just convinced that knowledge of how things are, what is what, is a subject for science (broadly understood) and philosophers have no business muscling into an area where they have no special competence. This sets him apart both from philosophers who believe it possible to discover fundamental facts about the world by pure intuition or other non-rational means and from philosophers who believe philosophical problems can be solved by appealing to scientific facts and theories. Like many philosophers at the time he was working, he heaps scorn on the truths metaphysicians profess to discover and the answers to philosophical problems tendered by naturalistic philosophers. And doubly so when it comes to colour. He denigrates the possibility of revealing facts about colour phenomena beyond what science tells us about them and thinks colour theory is wrongly invoked in answer to the problems of special interest to philosophers.

The riddles about colour that concern Wittgenstein are primarily conceptual in nature. He focuses on problems that arise about colour when one takes a step back and studies colour for its own sake. Focusing on how we talk and think about colour in everyday life, he takes it upon himself to untangle the knots we tie ourselves in when in a philosophical mood we reflect on our use of colour language. He does not disparage scrutiny of how scientists use colour language in their more technical inquiries but thinks these are too often a source of confusion. His efforts are orthogonal to the scientist's efforts inasmuch as he labours to elucidate the logical character of colour language and the necessities and possibilities it countenances rather than explore and explain empirical facts. What was, is, or will be the case where colour is concerned is not lost sight of. He is not exclusively concerned with words but holds rather that, in general, phenomena are incomprehensible without the intercession of language and endeavours to get clear about how colour language is properly used to talk about colour phenomena.

During the period Wittgenstein was seriously engaged in philosophy, roughly 1911 to 1951, it was mostly believed among the augurs – and firmly encouraged by Wittgenstein himself – that there is no such thing as synthetic a priori truth, that is, truth that is as informative as scientific truth and as necessary as logical truth. For Wittgenstein, as for a leading like-minded thinker: 'Science is the pursuit of Truth, and Philosophy is the pursuit of Meaning' (Schlick 1932: 367), and as another such thinker put it: 'The sciences aim at saying what is true about the world; philosophy aims at disclosing only the logic of what can be truly or even falsely said about the world' (Ryle 1967: 119). In Wittgenstein's view this goes for colour no less than for any other quality or property. Thus, when Moritz Schlick asked him, 'What answer can one give to a philosopher who believes that the statements of phenomenology are synthetic *a priori* judgements', he replied: 'It is indeed possible to make up words, but I cannot associate a thought with them' (WVC: 67–68). He invariably insisted judgements are either analytic a priori or synthetic a posteriori.

'A speck in a visual field … has, so to speak, a colour space around it'

Wittgenstein seems to have commented on the special character of colour first in 1916/1917. There is nothing to speak of on the subject early in *Notebooks 1914–1916*, the only remarks of any substance coming late in the book and near the start of the so-called *Prototractatus* (1915–1918), remarks later included in the *Tractatus* itself. Thus, Wittgenstein observes that 'a speck in a visual field need not be red but it must have a colour; it has, so to speak, a colour space [*Farbenraum*] around it' (PT, 2.0142, TLP, 2.0131). The burden of this important, if somewhat murky, remark is that colours (and colour concepts) form a system and are interrelated much as points in physical space (and spatial concepts) are interrelated. Wittgenstein's thought is that colours are associated with points in a space of colours no less than physical positions are associated with points in geometrical space. And likewise for other qualities and quantities. 'A tone', he adds, 'must have *a* pitch, the objects of sense *a* hardness, etc'. Without saying it in so many words he is taking tones to have a space of pitches around them, objects of sense to have a space of hardnesses around them, and similarly for other entities and attributes.

The abstract concept of a colour space (*Farbenraum*) introduced at 2.0131 of the *Tractatus* is closely allied with, if not modelled on, the mathematical physicist's conception of a phase space and the allied view of qualities and quantities as representable by means of coordinate systems, the most familiar of which is the system of Cartesian coordinates. (A phase space is a multidimensional space, the points of which represent the positions and momenta of particles or systems of particles.) It cannot be accidental that Wittgenstein also says at 2.0131: 'A spatial object must lie in infinite space. (A point in space is an argument place).'. He means that there is a function that yields for a given object or point in space – as argument – a location in physical or geometrical space – as value. (Compare the '+1'-function, which yields 2 as value given 1 as argument, 3 given 2, etc.) While Wittgenstein only mentions spatial points, he would have said the same for colours and he is naturally read as noting that just as 'This particle has such and such position' can be symbolized as 'p(a) = d' ('p' designating a position-function, 'a' the particle and 'd' its position), so 'This point is green' can be symbolized as 'c(p) = g' ('c' designating a colour-function', 'p' the point and 'g' its colour).

Other remarks in the *Tractatus* recycled from the *Prototractatus* echo the conception of colour and colour concepts sketched at 2.0131. At 2.0251, sixteen remarks later, Wittgenstein writes: 'Space, time and colour (colouredness) are forms of objects', that is, are necessarily coloured, necessarily have one of the possible colours in *Farbenraum*. (Here 'form' refers to the range of pertinent possibilities, and 'object' to common objects, not the simples that constitute the substance of the world, which are 'roughly speaking … colourless' (2.0232).) Also at 2.171 Wittgenstein says it is characteristic of 'the coloured [picture]' – that is, 'model of reality' (2.12) – that it 'can represent … everything coloured'. And at 4.123 he states that colours are essentially linked. He writes: 'A property is internal if it is unthinkable that its object does not possess it. (This blue colour and that stand in the internal relation of brighter and darker eo ipso. It is unthinkable that *these* two objects should not stand in this relation).' His point is that while the brightness of an object is a contingent fact about it – it could be more or less bright – a shade of a colour has to be brighter than a less bright one. Brightness is internal to colour just as magnitude is internal to numbers. A bright blue cannot be less bright than a less bright blue any more than 2 can be smaller than 1.

Given his early training and work in science and engineering (1906–1911), Wittgenstein would have been conversant with the strategy of exploiting a space of possibilities to represent position, time and other qualities and quantities. It is practically certain that he encountered this way of representing phenomena when reading Ludwig Boltzmann (1844–1906) on modern physics and Heinrich Hertz (1857–1894) on mechanics. (This may be in part why he placed Boltzmann and Hertz at the head of a list of influences he drew up in 1931; CV:16.) In any event the mathematical physicist's conception of representation is unmistakable in *Notebooks 1914–1916*. Thus Wittgenstein says: 'The method of symbolizing— is the system of coordinates which projects the situation into the proposition. The proposition corresponds to the fundamental coordinates. We might conceive two co-ordinates a_p and b_p as a proposition stating that the material point P is to be found in the place (ab)' (NB: 20; dated 29 October 1914). In addition he says: 'The fundamental co-ordinates together with the ordinates determine the points of a figure' (NB: 46; dated 8 May 1915) and says: 'Do not forget either that the picture may have very complicated co-ordinates to the world' (NB: 59; dated 13 June 1915, also compare NB: 16, 48, 64 and 69).

The remarks in the *Tractatus* (and *Notebooks 1914–1916*) in which the mathematical physicist's conception of representation are to the fore have received less close examination than the remarks in the *Tractatus* (and *Notebooks 1914–1916*) in which the logician's conception of representation is front and centre. It mostly goes unnoticed that the 2.1s and 2.2s, commonly cited as source of 'the picture theory of meaning', are devoted to representation no less than the 2.0s. Nor is it much appreciated that at 3.032 Wittgenstein compares contradictions in logic with the coordinates of points that do not exist, at 3.41 says: 'The propositional sign and logical coordinates: that is logical space', and at 4.04 declares – with a nod to Hertz – that 'the proposition [and] the state of affairs, which it represents, ... must both have the same logical (mathematical) multiplicity'. Nor again are the remarks on scientific representation at 6.341, one of the longest entries in the book, read as squaring with the conception of representation informing 2.0131, 3.032, 3.41 and 4.04. Wittgenstein not only notes that 'mechanics determines a form of description', he also expressly states that 'as with the system of numbers one must be able to write down any arbitrary number, so with the system of mechanics one must be able to write down any arbitrary physical proposition'. For him, as he observes in the same number, describing a phenomenon by mechanics is comparable to describing an arrangement of spots by placing a net over it and specifying which of its squares coincide with a spot, which not.

' ... for it is excluded by the logical structure of colour'

After defending the proposition that 'mechanics determine a form of description' at 6.341, Wittgenstein takes up the celebrated problem of accounting for colour incompatibility, that is, why no point can be red and green, say, at the same time. At 6.3751 he states that the impossibility is logical, not factual, and sets about providing an explanation that shows that the possibility of two colours occurring together is logically excluded, an explanation that has been judged time and again to come up short, indeed to be the Achilles' heel of the *Tractatus*. Wittgenstein cannot, it is maintained, justifiably hold that 'the assertion that a point in the visual field has two different colours at the same time, is a contradiction' given the account of logic developed in the rest of the book. The problem is that there are no better examples of elementary propositions than 'A is red' and 'A is green' (where 'A' names a point in the visual field), a fact that clashes irreconcilably with the claim in the third paragraph of the number that 'the logical product [i.e. the conjunction] of two elementary propositions can neither be a tautology nor a contradiction'.

The much-stressed claim that Wittgenstein fails to show that the joint occurrence of two colours is logically contradictory and the 'later philosophy' is traceable to his having realized he had stumbled is easily comprehended but hard to swallow. Leaving aside that he stated earlier in the *Tractatus* that he could not specify an elementary proposition (5.5571), there is the awkward fact that taking him to have faltered regarding colour incompatibility requires taking him to have faltered regarding pitch incompatibility, hardness incompatibility and all other pairs of determinates for the same determinable. And arguably still worse, the alleged problem would arise for mass, position, velocity and other quantities of mechanics, something Wittgenstein would surely have noticed and attempted to take care of. Nor should it be overlooked that Russell had provided in *Principles of Mathematics*, a book Wittgenstein knew well, essentially the same solution to the problem without provoking an unfavourable response (1937 [1903]: 467).

Wittgenstein is certainly in trouble if 'This point is red' is a prime candidate for an elementary proposition and the conjunction of elementary propositions cannot be a contradiction. Before dismissing what he says at 6.3751, however, the explanation of the impossibility advanced in the first paragraph merits a closer look. In this paragraph Wittgenstein says: 'For two colours, e.g. to be at one place in the visual field, is impossible, logically impossible, for it is excluded by the logical structure of colour.' His thought is twofold. He is noting that colour is logically structured and it is its logical structure that precludes two colours occurring together. This comports well with the conception of representation adumbrated at 2.0131 and adjacent remarks that different colours are differently located in colour space and hence cannot – as a matter of logic – be at the same place at the same time or other determinates of the same determinable. In each case the problem of incompatibility is resolved by drawing attention to how qualities and quantities are represented. As Wittgenstein later puts it: 'The truth is, *two* determinations of the same kind (co-ordinate) are impossible' (PR: 112).

Reading Wittgenstein as tracing colour incompatibility to the logical structure of colour jibes with Merrill and Jaakko Hintikka's contention that 'attributions of different perceptual qualities are intrinsically single-valued, i.e., represented logically speaking by genuine functions', a view they take to be 'forcefully asserted by Wittgenstein in 2.0131' (1986: 123). As the Hintikkas understand the situation, 'the logical incompatibility of two-colour ascriptions ... is shown by their logical representation in the usual logical notation: a function cannot have two different values for the same argument because of its "logical" form, i.e., because of its logical type'. (Taking 'C' to abbreviate 'a has colour ... ' and treating the quantifiers as specified at TLP 5.5321, 'This point is red and green' – i.e. 'c(a) = r & c(a) = g' – becomes 'Cr & Cg & ¬(∃x,y)(Cx & Cy)', a clear-cut contradiction.) The sole difficulty, if the Hintikkas are to be believed, is that Wittgenstein does not commit himself to the view they sketch. They only allow that 'from an ahistorical, systematic viewpoint, it looks as if [he] were committed to such a construal of the general concept of colour' (1986: 124). True, 'the historical truth seems to be that [he] never spelled out the mapping construal of colours', at least not explicitly. He is, however, naturally and reasonably regarded as having tacitly 'assented to [the construal] verbally'.

When Wittgenstein is understood as suggested, the second paragraph of 6.3751 falls into place. Contrary to how this is routinely read Wittgenstein does not suppose that 'This is red' is subject to physical analysis. There is nothing in the text to suggest that he believed 'the apparently simple concepts red, blue (supposing us to mean by those words absolutely specific shades) are really complex and formally incompatible', still less that he attempted 'to show how this may be, by analysing them in terms of vibrations' (Ramsey 1923: 473). To be sure, such an analysis only reduces 'the difficulty to that of the *necessary* properties of space, time, and matter or the ether', properties 'hardly capable of further reduction of this kind'. But far from suggesting how attributions of more than one colour to the same point should be analysed, Wittgenstein invites us to consider an analogous case. He goes on to say: 'Let us consider how this contradiction presents itself in physics. Somewhat as follows: That a particle cannot at the same time have two velocities, *i.e.* that at the same time it cannot be in two places, *i.e.* that particles in different places at the same time cannot be identical.' His point in the paragraph is that, as he says, the contradiction also occurs in physics.

'The very fundamental part of the subject'

The suggestion that the argument of 6.3751 sounds the death knell of the *Tractatus* is not lacking in textual support. While Wittgenstein's commitment to the mathematical physicist's conception of representation is hard to deny, it is harder still to ignore his commitment to the logician's conception of representation (and the thought that 'This is red and green' can be symbolized by 'R & G', where 'R' and 'G' hold places for 'This is red' and 'This is green'). If, as Wittgenstein has it, propositions can be obtained from elementary propositions by repeated application of the 'N-operator', i.e. the 'neither . . . nor . . . ' operator (6–6.001), and elementary propositions are logically independent, that is, do not contradict one another (4.211), there is little possibility of showing 'This is red and green' is a contradiction, and Ramsey is on firm ground when he states that the proposition cannot be the negation of a 'formal tautology' (1923: 473). There are just two possibilities (granting that 'A is red' is elementary if 'A is green' and vice versa). Were 'A is red' and 'A is green' elementary, they could be jointly true and 'A is red and green' would not be a contradiction. But if they are non-elementary, they are analysable and, as Ramsey says, 'the difficulty [would reduce] to that of the *necessity* [other] properties'.

Before concluding that Wittgenstein has merely put off the evil day, however, it needs to be considered how representation figures in the *Tractatus* and what exactly the argument of 6.3751 is. Accepting that colour incompatibility – along with position incompatibility, velocity incompatibility, et cetera – is readily explained given the mathematical physicist's conception of representation, it only remains to consider how this conception is related to the logician's conception and correlatively how mathematical impossibility is related to logical impossibility. While Wittgenstein seems to criticize the reduction of mathematics to logic in the *Tractatus*, he also seems to have believed that mathematics is in the final analysis nothing but logic. His friend David Pinsent recorded in his diary on 25 August 1913 that he was not concerned with Russell's 'purely Mathematical work – for instance most of his "Principia"', only with 'the very fundamental part of the subject' (1990: 59). And it is likely that – along with most other interested parties at the time – he continued to embrace the reduction in 1918 when compiling the *Tractatus*. It is one thing to criticize Russell's treatment of the matter and fail to rescue it, another to have rejected his conclusion and believe it cannot be rescued.

Focusing on how Wittgenstein would have taken mathematics to be related to logic (and setting aside his criticism of Russell's definition of numbers and treatment of mathematical induction), he is best understood as believing math-ematical impossibility is at root identical to logical impossibility (and the mathematical conception of representation is of a piece with the logician's conception). Though well short of clinching the matter, it cannot be fortuitous that he says: 'Mathematics is a logical method' (6.2), 'The logic of the world which the propositions of logic show in tautologies, mathematics shows in equations' (6.22), and 'Mathematics is a method of logic' (6.34). While these remarks can be interpreted as pointing in the opposite direction, they lend support to the suggestion that Wittgenstein was taking mathematics to be to all intents and purposes an extension of logic when he spoke in 6.3751 of the joint occurrence of two colours as 'impossible, logically impossible' and suggested that 'this contradiction' occurs in physics. Had he repudiated the reduction lock, stock and barrel, why would he have referred to the 'logical structure of colour' rather than its mathematical structure, spoken of 'logical impossibility' instead of 'mathematical impossibility' and observed that the 'contradiction presents itself in physics'?

The proposed interpretation of 6.3751 is not ruled out by remarks in the *Tractatus* that may seem, at first glance, at variance with logic as viewed there. It is no objection that mathematics cannot by any stretch of the imagination be regarded as an extension of the logic of sentence connectives 'and' and 'not' (or 'neither . . . nor . . . ') or, more liberally, as an extension of the quantifier logic that makes provision for 'all' and 'some' (compare 6). At 5.501, arguably a more important remark than 6, Wittgenstein opts for a view of logic that comprehends mathematics of the sort he would have taken to figure in physics. Nor is it a deadly strike against reading Wittgenstein as embracing the logistic reduction that he says logic comprises tautologies (6.1) and mathematics equations (6.2). He had a much broader notion of tautology than the notion generally accepted today and treated them as often as not as propositions that convey no information (see Dreben and Floyd 1991). Moreover at 6.24 he prevaricates and states that mathematical identities can be regarded as 'equations that express the substitutability of two expressions'. The third paragraph of 6.3751 was drafted later than the other two, and his remarks about logical independence at 4.211 and 5.134 may have been at the time front of mind, not colour incompatibility.

It is worth noting too that Wittgenstein's suggestion that colour incompatibility is due to 'the logical structure of colour' was not seriously challenged in the immediate aftermath of the publication of the *Tractatus*. Since Russell had provided much the same account in *Principles of Mathematics* it makes sense that he passed over 6.3751 without comment in his 'Introduction' to the *Tractatus*. And still more surprising, perhaps, Wittgenstein, ever alert to his own errors, never subsequently mentioned the difficulty himself. Nor again should it be overlooked that, after going through the book remark-by-remark with Wittgenstein in Austria some months after composing his review of the *Tractatus*, Ramsey seems to have come to think it was he, not Wittgenstein, who had erred. When elaborating what he took to be the vision adumbrated in the *Tractatus* in the years that followed, he did not allude to, let alone repeat, the criticism he pressed in his review. In fact he seems to have embraced the mathematical physicist's conception of representation. Thus in 'Theories' he says: 'Of the terms in our primary system [i.e. the language we start with] not merely some but even all may be best symbolized by numbers. For instance, colours have a structure, in which any given colour can be assigned a place by three numbers' (1990 [1929]: 113).

Other Discussions and Further Reading

Rothhaupt (1996) is a philological study of Wittgenstein's treatment of colour concepts early and late. For philosophical treatments of colour perpendicular to Wittgenstein's treatment of the logic of colour concepts, the question of whether colour exists, whether colours are subjective or objective, whether they are occurrent, dispositional or relational properties, etc., see Maund (2018). For criticisms of Wittgenstein's treatment of colour concepts from a naturalistic point of view see Westphal 1987 and Hardin 1988, and Lugg 2017b for pushback. For Wittgenstein and phenomenology see Monk 2014, and for yet other treatments of Wittgenstein on colour, see Silva 2017. On the suggestion that logical space (*Tractatus* 1.13) is comparable to phase space, see Preston 2015. For more on *Tractatus* 2.0131, see Black 1964: 50–55 and Griffin 1964: 99–108. For Wittgenstein's debt to Hertz and Boltzmann, see Preston 2017. For more on *Tractatus* 6.341, see Mounce 1981: Chapter 7 and McGuinness 2002: Chapter 11. For more on *Tractatus* 6.3751 and colour exclusion as a problem for Wittgenstein in the *Tractatus*, see Black 1964: 367–369, Hacker 1986: 108ff, Child 2011: 44, and Klagge 2022: 277–278 in addition to Ramsey 1923. For the fact that Russell anticipates Wittgenstein's treatment of colour incompatibility, see Landini 2007: 86, and Lugg 2015a: 50ff. Von Wright 1996: 10–13 and Moss 2012: 842–845 also treat Wittgenstein on colour exclusion sympathetically. For Wittgenstein's criticism of Russell's 'logicism', see Goldfarb 2018: 241–245.

2 Wittgenstein on Colour, 1929–1930

'The number is a means of representation'

Wittgenstein returned to Cambridge in January 1929 and began composing (or redrafting) remarks on a variety of topics, colour included. His discussion is not easy to follow but it is pretty clear that during the first months of the year he came to see that the geometry of the visual field differs from Euclidean geometry, that is, the geometry of physical space, the only sort of geometry he had considered in the *Tractatus* (MS 105:1–3; also 45). This in turn seems to have prompted him to think arithmetic belongs to the base of language, not its superstructure. Thus he asks: 'How can the shape of a fleck in the visual field be described? Can coordinate geometry be done in the visual field?' (MS 105: 9). Whereas in the *Tractatus* he declares: 'The logical forms [of propositions] are anumerical' (4.128), he now says: 'I am apparently thrown back against my will on arithmetic. The number is a means of representation' (MS 105: 19). He has come to see that propositions, elementary propositions included, may be numerical, that is, may include number words and hence be logically interrelated.

While still able to regard the attribution of colour to points in visual space as representable by points in colour space, he has to accept that such propositions, even when analysed, may not be logically independent.

The remarks about colour Wittgenstein drafted in the early months of 1929 are not without interest but pale in comparison with the remarks on the topic in 'Some Remarks on Logical Form', a paper intended for, but not presented at, the Aristotelean Society meeting in July 1929. In this paper Wittgenstein is widely read as holding that the argument of the *Tractatus* falls short because it fails to account for degrees of a quality (see Kenny 1973: 104–105; Soames 2003: 237–239; also Child 2011: 77–78). The key remark is reckoned to be: 'The proposition E($2b$), which says that E has two units of brightness' cannot be analysed as 'E(b) & E(b)' or as 'E(b') & E(b'')', the former being logically equivalent to 'E(b)', the latter leaving open the question of which unit of brightness E would have if it had just one degree of brightness, b' or b'' (RLF: 33). This is an implausible interpretation if only because it beggars belief that Wittgenstein would have thought two rather crude analyses undermine the *Tractatus*, much less prove 'the statement which attributes a degree to a quality cannot further be analysed, and ... the relation of difference of degree is an internal relation'. Nor is it likely that, when compiling the *Tractatus*, he had overlooked that Newtonian mechanics recognizes degrees of mass, velocity and acceleration and 'E has two degrees of brightness' is logically comparable to 'E has two units of momentum'.

In 'Some Remarks on Logical Form', which – as the title indicates – deals with the structure of propositions, Wittgenstein begins by noting that 'we get a picture of the pure form if we abstract from the meaning of the single words, or symbols (so far as they have independent meanings)' and that the analysis of a proposition must eventually 'come to a point where it reaches propositional forms which are not themselves composed of simpler propositional forms', a task he concedes 'philosophy has hardly yet begun to tackle ... at some points' (RLF: 29). Then, after more stage-setting, he offers his 'first definite remark on the logical analysis of actual phenomena', namely that 'for their representation numbers (rational and irrational) must enter the structure of atomic [i.e. elementary] propositions themselves' (RLF: 31). In particular he writes: 'Numbers will have to enter [the forms of atomic propositions] when – as we should say in ordinary language – we are dealing with properties which admit of gradation' (RLF: 32) and adds: 'The statement which attributes a degree to a quality' – for example, 'E has two degrees of brightness' – cannot be 'further analysed' (RLF: 33). This is not proved, only stated. Perhaps accepting a conclusion he had come to earlier, Wittgenstein simply adds that 'E($2b$)' cannot be analysed as 'E(b) & E(b)' or 'E(b') & E(b'')'.

When numbers are taken to enter the structure of elementary propositions, the question arises of how the 'exclusion' of 'A is blue' and 'A is red' is represented 'in symbolism' (RLF: 34). Wittgenstein allows it is 'a deficiency of our notation that it does not prevent the formation of such nonsensical constructions' and ends up noting that the requisite rules of syntax 'will have to tell us that in the case of certain kinds of atomic propositions described in terms of definite symbolic features [,] certain combinations of [truth possibilities] must be left out' (RLF: 35). In a 'perfect notation', something that 'as we all know, has not yet been achieved', 'A is blue and A is red' will, Wittgenstein observes, be expressed differently from the conjunction of non-contradictory propositions; that is, it will by virtue of a rule of syntax turn out to be a contradiction. The trouble is that the rules of syntax 'cannot be laid down until we have reached the ultimate analysis of the phenomena in question [including, presumably, colour]'. This is debatable. Can we be sure that there are, as Wittgenstein intimates, 'definite rules of syntax' that exclude 'such nonsensical constructions'? (Could this have been, in part at least, what prompted him to disown the paper and choose to speak at the Aristotelean Society about generality and infinity in mathematics?)

The mathematical conception of representation is not trumpeted in 'Some remarks on logic form' but neither it is absent. Wittgenstein writes in line with the conception: 'If, now, we try to get at an actual analysis [of propositions of ordinary language] ... we meet with the forms of space and time [,] with the whole manifold of spatial and temporal objects, as colours, sounds, etc., etc., with their gradations, continuous transitions, and combinations' (RLF: 31). (Compare TLP 2.0121: 'We cannot think of spatial objects at all apart from space, or temporal objects apart from time'.) As 'a simple example', Wittgenstein suggests, 'the representation of patch P by the expression "[6–9, 3–8]" and ... a proposition about it, *e.g.*, P is red by the symbol "[6–9, 3–8]R"' (RLF: 31–32; 'R' is 'yet an unanalysed term' and '(6,3)', '(9,3)', '(9,8)' and '(6,8)' coordinates of the patch). There is an echo here of Wittgenstein's comparison in *Tractatus* 6.341 of Newtonian mechanics with a network of squares. And in agreement with the mathematical physicist's conception of representation, he says: 'That which corresponds in reality to the function '()PT' leaves room for only one entity' (RLF: 33), '()PT' designating a function that associates a colour with a given patch at a given time.

'The elementary colours [are] very pointed'

Back in Vienna at the end of 1929, Wittgenstein returned in discussion with Friedrich Waismann and Moritz Schlick to the question of the nature of 'the colour-system' and the representation of colour. In Schlick's home, on 25 December, he apparently stated that propositions stand and fall in groups rather than individually. 'Once', he is quoted as saying: 'I wrote, "A proposition is laid against reality like a ruler. Only the end-points of the graduating lines actually *touch* the object that is to be measured". I now prefer to say that a *system of propositions* is laid against reality like a ruler. ... I lay *all the graduating lines* against it at the same time' (WVC: 63–64; compare TLP 2.1511–2.15121). Moreover Wittgenstein is reported to have added: 'If I say, for instance, that this or that point in the visual field is *blue*, then I know not merely that, but also that [it] is not green, not red, not yellow, etc. I have laid the entire colour-scale against [the point] at one go. This is also the reason why a point cannot have different colours. ... When I lay a system of propositions against reality. ... there is only *one* state of affairs that can exist, not several— just as in the spatial case' (WVC: 64, also compare WVC: 89).

Supplementing the idea of a space of colours with the picture of laying a system of propositions against reality clarifies the conception of colour as logically structured presented at 6.3751 in the *Tractatus*. It explains why the joint occurrence of two colours is 'excluded by the logical structure of colour' and obviates the need to explain the impossibility, as in 'Some Remarks on Logical Form', by postulating that the truth table for the conjunction of the two colours has three rather than four lines and deeming the case in which both conjuncts are true excluded by a 'rule of syntax'. In addition the representation of orange, purple and other immediate colours is readily accounted for despite the impossibility of the occurrence of two colours at the same place. Colour incompatibility is no barrier to orange being a mixture of red and yellow or purple being a mixture of red and blue. Orange and purple occupy different positions in colour space from their component colours. (Also recall that the colour spectrum has orange between red and yellow and purple between red and blue.) This is not at odds with the conception of *Farbenraum* in the *Tractatus*, only unmentioned (or unnoticed). What is different is that Wittgenstein recognizes that 'colour space' and the 'problem of colour' are more complex than he had earlier stated.

While the possibility of the joint occurrence of some pairs of colours – red and yellow, for instance – is readily explained given the conception of *Farbenraum* mentioned in the *Tractatus*, the impossibility of the joint occurrence of some other pairs of colours – red and green, for instance – poses a problem. (Recall that red and green are not adjacent on the colour spectrum.) Wittgenstein seems never to have accepted the possibility of a mixture of red and green comparable to orange. Without doubt he would have resisted the popular suggestion that leaves in autumn are a mixture of red and green as opposed to green with red specks and would not have looked kindly on reports in leading scientific journals of experiments that a mixture of red and green is physically possible, even perceivable in special circumstances. Certainly he would not have agreed that there is no mixture of red and green because nothing can be two colours at once, it being arguable by a parallel argument that orange is not a mixture of red and yellow. Nor again would he have been satisfied with declaring a mixture of red and green logically impossible because 'it is excluded by the logical structure of colour' (*Tractatus* 6.3751). This merely defers the problem. To complete the job it has to be explained why a mixture of red and green is excluded but not a mixture of red and yellow.

What is it about the space of colours that explains the difference between the possibility of the one sort of mixture and the impossibility of the other? In 1929/1930 Wittgenstein considers for the first time how exactly colour space is structured and how the points representing the colours are interrelated. In the *Tractatus* he only stated that colour is logically structured, and one can be forgiven for thinking he took it to be no more structured than position; that is, he had inadvertently assumed that, just as every point in Euclidean space represents a possible position, so every point in colour space represents a possible colour. What is required, once the impossibility of certain 'intermediate colours' is noticed, is an acknowledgement of the fact that *Farbenraum* is more highly structured than stated in the *Tractatus*. Only latish in 1929 did Wittgenstein take up the question of how colour space is structured and state, rather cryptically, in conversation with Schlick and Waismann on 22 December that 'the elementary colours [are] very pointed' and provide – without recorded explanation – a diagram illustrating 'the form of the colour-body' (WVC: 42). (In this connection it is worth noting that in subsequent conversations he refers to the structure of visual space as non-Euclidean (WVC: 59) and states that 'in geometry we are never dealing with reality but only with spatial possibilities' (WVC: 63).)

Wittgenstein is, however, more transparently committed to the mathematical physicist's conception of representation in 1929/1930 than in 1918. As Russell notes in a report he prepared on Wittgenstein's progress at the time, the notion of *Farbenraum* was now front and centre in his thinking. Though benefitting from just five days of conversation with Wittgenstein in mid-March and late April 1930 and only managing to read a third of a collection of remarks Wittgenstein prepared to bring him up to date on what he was doing, Russell saw that Wittgenstein exploits the idea of 'a collection of possibilities', calls such a collection a 'space', speaks of 'a "space" of colours and a "space" of sounds', and conscripts 'the word "grammar" to cover what corresponds in language to these various "spaces"' (WC: 183, letter dated 8 May 1930). While disinclined to recognize 'Wittgenstein's theories' as true and hoping they are not, Russell grants that they are 'novel, very original, and indubitably important', in fact 'may easily prove to constitute a whole new philosophy' (WC: 440).

Had Russell forgotten that the notion of a space figures not only in the *Tractatus* but also in his own much earlier *Principles of Mathematics* (see especially 467–468 on colour and 494–498 on 'Hertz's Dynamics')?

'The colour octahedron … is a grammatical representation, not a psychological one'

In *Philosophical Remarks*, a rearrangement of the material Wittgenstein produced for Russell (compiled in 1930; German text 1964; English translation 1975), colour is treated more systematically than in the *Tractatus* and 'Some Remarks on Logical Form'. After a few remarks about analysis, representation and what is essential to our language, Wittgenstein stresses that physics is very different from what he refers to as phenomenology. Echoing a point he had stressed in discussion with Schlick and Waismann on 25 December 1929 (WVC: 63), he writes: 'Physics … is concerned to establish laws. Phenomenology only establishes the possibilities. Thus, phenomenology would be the grammar of the description of those facts on which physics builds its theories' (PR §1). This suggestion – that phenomenology understood as concerning possibilities (and grammar) is altogether different from physics (and any other science) – is central to Wittgenstein's treatment of colour, in fact his thinking in general. There is, he is reiterating, no subject straddling science and logic, no such thing as synthetic a priori knowledge and truth, for him the hallmark of metaphysics. Setting aside science, which Wittgenstein takes to fall outside the philosopher's bailiwick, there is only grammar understood as a system of rules of language for the description of facts, facts about colour included.

Having distinguished between grammar and physical fact, Wittgenstein provides what he describes as 'a *rough* representation of colour-space' (PR §1). He notes that the relationships among the colours are condensed in the colour octahedron, 'an octahedron with the pure colours at the corner-points'. (More specifically the colour octahedron is a double pyramid with red, yellow, green and blue at the base, black and white at the apexes.) It is unclear why Wittgenstein says the colour octahedron is 'a *rough* representation'. (He may be allowing for the fact that it makes no provision for brown, beige, florescent pink, etc. Subsequently he speaks of the representation without qualification'.) No doubt, however, his central thought is that the colour octahedron is comparable to a diagram displaying the relations between above and below, in front and behind, and at the right and at the left. Both representations summarize logical structure and indicate what can and cannot be meaningfully said, in the one case, the possibility of something being in front and to the right of something else but not its being in front and behind it, in the other case the possibility of a mixture of red and yellow but not one of red and green. (Note that red and yellow are adjacent colours, red and green opposed colours. Also compare the colour wheel with red at 0°, blue at 90°, green at 180° and yellow at 270°. This is a still rougher representation of colour.)

Wittgenstein was not the first to take the colour octahedron to summarize relations among the colours. For instance Alois Höfler (1853–1928), the Austrian educational theorist and philosopher (also a student of Boltzmann's), introduced the colour octahedron in his textbook *Psychologie* (1897). It seems, however, that Wittgenstein was the first to regard the colour octahedron as summarizing the grammar of colour concepts and treat the relationships among the colours summarized as comparable to the relationships among positions summarized by Euclidean geometry. As he says in *Philosophical Remarks*: 'The words "Colour", "Sound", "Number", etc could appear in the chapter headings of our grammar' (§3). For him: 'The colour octahedron ... is a grammatical representation, not a psychological one' (§1). '[It] is grammar, since it says that you can speak of reddish blue but not of reddish green, etc' (§39). (Also he again equates phenomenology with grammar, that is, takes it to concern what is intelligibly sayable. 'Isn't', he asks (§4), 'the theory of harmony at least in part phenomenology and therefore grammar?')

The treatment of colour in *Philosophical Remarks*, like the treatment in the *Tractatus*, accords the notion of colour space and the logical structure of colour pride of place. But it is significantly different and hints at what is to come. The idea of expressing the concepts of a department of language in an easily grasped form is floated in the *Tractatus* but the colour octahedron is Wittgenstein's first explicit discussion of how colour is logically structured. In fact in the first section of *Philosophical Remarks* Wittgenstein adds a point about philosophy he evidently deemed enormously important, namely: 'The octahedron as a representation [*Oktaeder-Darstellung*] is a *surveyable* representation [übersichtliche *Darstellung*] of the grammatical rules. Above all our grammar lacks *surveyability* [Übersichtlichkeit]' (PR §1; translation modified). This remark heralds one of the more famous thoughts Wittgenstein expresses in the *Investigations*: 'A main source of our failure to understand is that we don't have *an overview* of the use of our words. – Our grammar is deficient in surveyability. ... The concept of a surveyable representation [*übersichtlichen Darstellung*] is of fundamental significance for us. It characterizes the way we represent things, how we look at matters' (PI §122).

To regard the colour octahedron as a grammatical representation is to focus on colour as such (and colour concepts). As Wittgenstein stresses in *Philosophical Remarks*, the topic under discussion is 'colour itself, and not pigment, light, process on or in the retina, etc' (PR §218). When examining colour from the standpoint of grammar or language, he is not, he repeats, 'of course speaking about pigments' (§220). There is a world of difference, one he frequently highlights, between mentioning the colour red and describing a pigment or light as red. (See, e.g., PI §57: 'Certainly it makes no sense to say that the colour red (as opposed to the pigment) is torn up or pounded to bits'.) This difference must, Wittgenstein thinks, be kept firmly in mind, especially in philosophy, since forgetting it is apt to cause no end of mischief. Conflating colours with what has colour and treating logical questions about colour as empirical questions about pigments or light often results in misunderstanding, confusion, or worse. (Also note that in the so-called *Urfassung* Wittgenstein writes, '*die Farbe Rot* (*color, nämlich, nicht pigmentum*)' (PU §55) and deprecates the 'confusion of colour with pigment [*Verwechslung von color & pigmentum*]' (PU §123).)

'The concept of an "elementary proposition" now loses all of its earlier significance'

In the balance of *Philosophical Remarks* Wittgenstein returns several times to the question of how 'colour' is used and the nature of *Farbenraum*. He declares the question: 'Can someone who doesn't know what red and green are like, really see what we (or I) call "blue" and "yellow"?' to be 'just as nonsensical as the question whether someone else with normal vision really sees the same as I do' (§41), writes (referring to the idea of a space of colours and the mathematical conception of representation): 'Grey must already be conceived as being in lighter/darker space if we want to talk of its being possible for it to get darker or lighter' (§42), and adds: 'A black colour can become lighter but not louder. That means it is in light/dark space but not loud/soft space' (§45). Moreover, noting that he had his present view much earlier, he says: 'When I built language up by using a coordinate system for representing a state of affairs in space, I introduced into language an element it doesn't normally use. This is surely permissible. ... The written sign without the coordinate system is senseless. Mustn't we then use something similar for representing colours?' (§46). (In an editor's note (PR: 349), Rush Rhees suggests Wittgenstein is referring to 'Some Remarks on Logical Form', but he could just as well have been referring to the *Tractatus* since the notion of a coordinate system also figures there.)

In Chapter VIII of *Philosophical Remarks*, Wittgenstein revisits the problem of explaining colour incompatibility. He notes it will not do to point out that 'two colours in one place simply combine to make [a third colour]', there being no good answer to the question of what red and green make (§76). (Of course he is not denying that red and green pigments combine to make black.)

Indeed it is, Wittgenstein observes, even misleading to say that two colours cannot occur simultaneously at the same place since this seems to imply 'red and green … are as a matter of fact never together' whereas – as a matter of logic – 'you can't even say they are together, or, consequently that they are never together' (§78; also see §77). On the other hand it makes good sense to say of two red-blues: 'There is an even redder blue than the redder of these two. That is to say, from the given I can construct what is not given. You could say the colours have an elementary affinity with one another' (§76). What has to go is not the Tractarian claim that some colour combinations are logically excluded but only the assumption that every elementary proposition is logically independent of every other such proposition, 'a construction … within the elementary proposition' being perfectly possible. This being so, Wittgenstein concludes: 'The concept of an "elementary proposition" now loses all of its earlier significance' (§83).

Part of the problem with the conception of elementary proposition presupposed in the *Tractatus* is that the analogy of a proposition (or picture) as a yardstick or scale [*Masstab*] limps (2.1512). 'It isn't', Wittgenstein writes (repeating what he said in December 1929 in Vienna), 'a proposition which I put against reality as a yardstick, it's a *system* of propositions … In my old conception of an elementary proposition there was no determination of the value of a coordinate [i.e., the conception was divorced from the notion of colour space]; although my remark that a coloured body is in a colour-space, etc., should have put me straight on to this. A coordinate of reality may be only be determined *once*' (PR §§82–83). What Wittgenstein says he missed was that 'we are dealing with yardsticks, not in some fashion with isolated graduation marks' (§84). Does this settle the matter? Granting 'it's *impossible* to set one scale simultaneously at two graduation marks' does not suffice by itself to explain why reddish yellow is permitted, reddish green precluded. (Wittgenstein seems less than fully content with his new way of viewing the matter since at §40, which was drafted later than §§82–84, he asks: 'How far can you compare the colours with points on a scale? Can you say that the direction leading from black to red is a different one from the one you must take from black to blue?')

The penultimate chapter of *Philosophical Remarks*, Chapter XXI (§§218–224), is devoted to 'phenomenological colour theory [*phänomenologische Farbenlehre*]' (§218). What he is seeking, Wittgenstein notes, is an account of the grammar of colour, 'not a physical and equally not a physiological [theory]'. (I take his follow-up remark – 'It must be a theory in *pure* phenomenology in which mention is only made of what is actually perceptible and in which no hypothetical objects – waves, rods, cones and all that – occur' – to be of a piece with his view of phenomenology as grammar.) Moreover he thinks 'we can recognize colours as mixtures of red, green, blue, yellow, white and black *immediately*', where 'this is still always the colour itself, and not pigment, light, process on or in the retina, etc'. What is much less clear is whether there is 'a metric for colours', and whether there is 'a sense in saying, for instance, that with respect to the amount of red in it one colour is *halfway* between two other colours'. It is not obvious that there is no such metric but, after exploring the possibility of one, Wittgenstein ends up unconvinced. 'I have', he concludes, 'no grounds for saying of either [two different shades of orange] that it is closer to red than yellow. – There simply isn't a "midpoint" here' (§220). 'The concepts "closer to" and "further from" are simply of no use at all or are misleading when we apply these phrases' (§221).

Wittgenstein also has a number of other useful remarks on the logic of colour concepts elsewhere in *Philosophical Remarks*. He wonders whether it could make sense to say: 'That's not a noise, it's a colour?' (PR §8), writes: 'If I can only see something black and say it isn't red, how do I know that I am not talking nonsense?' (§39), and asks why if four-dimensional space is believed imaginable, 'why not also … colours which in addition to the degree of saturation, hue and intensity of light, are susceptible to being determined in yet a fourth way' (§66). Furthermore he observes that 'a yellow tinge is not the colour yellow' (§80) and declares that there are just four primaries, red, blue, green and yellow, white and black aside (§114). If someone says 'there are 5 pure colours, in that case we don't understand him, or must suppose we completely misunderstand one another', the number being 'demarcated in dictionaries and grammar and not within language'. How many pure colours there are is not information properly so-called but integral to our means of conveying information. As Wittgenstein sees it, 'the proposition "*A* has a pure colour" simply means "*A* is red, or yellow, or green, or blue' (§116). In fact he is, he confesses, inclined to think 'the things themselves are … the four basic colours, space, time and other [such givens]' (§147).

Other Discussions and Further Reading

For a 'critical interpretation of "Some Remarks on Logic Form"' pivoting on Ramsey's 1923 objection, see Jacquette 1988: 153–192, especially 161–164 and 172–181. I examine the paper paragraph-by-paragraph in Lugg 2015b: 14–17. For Wittgenstein's remarks on colour 1929–1930 see Engelmann 2013 and 2017, and Kuusela 2023. For more on Wittgenstein's *Philosophical Remarks* and the circuitous composition of the published material, see Paul 2007: Chapter 1 and Engelmann 2018: section 2, and

2020. It is central to the interpretation of Wittgenstein's remarks defended here that he is concerned with colour concepts, that is, colour logically rather than empirically construed, and is wrongly read as treating the physics, physiology or psychology of colour or concerned with the phenomenology of colour (except insofar as this is equated with grammar). For more on the alleged existence of 'forbidden colours' and the possibility, stoutly defended in some quarters, of creating a mixture of red and green in the laboratory by stabilizing red and green lights on subjects' retinas, see Lugg 2017b and 2021: 8–9.

3 Wittgenstein on Colour, 1930–1939

'What we are doing is giving … grammatical rules and conventions'

Not unexpectedly, when Wittgenstein began teaching in January 1930 at Cambridge University, he reprised thoughts about colour already recorded in *Philosophical Remarks*. Thus he is reported to have said: 'Colours are imagined placed on octahedron. This is really part of grammar. … "People under these circumstances have red after-images" is psychology. But "There is such a colour as greenish-blue", is phenomenology, or grammar' (MWL:16–17; also LWL: 8). And, when discussing the impossibility of 'a mixture of orange and purple', he apparently again noted that he is concerned with 'colours, not pigments' (LWL: 11), that is, with colour itself, not with paint, ink or light. Moreover he reportedly said: 'There are four primary colours' means 'There are red, blue, green and yellow' (LWL: 12). This is a point about usage. He is not denying that black and white are often counted as primaries, only challenging views of the sort championed by Newton in the *Optiks* (1704), according to which orange, indigo and violet are primaries along with red, yellow, green and blue, and the eminent colour theorist, A.H. Munsell, according to which purple is a fifth primary. Nor, incidentally, is he disputing that in the case of paints just red, yellow and blue count as primaries, in the case of lights just red, green and blue or blue-violet.

G.E. Moore, who was attending the lectures, reports that he was surprised that Wittgenstein 'spent a good deal of time in discussing what would usually be called a question about colours, namely, the question of how the four "saturated" colours, pure yellow, pure red, pure blue and pure green … are distinguished from those "saturated" colours which are not "primary"' (Moore 1993: 108). In retrospect, however, this is hardly surprising. Wittgenstein had only recently come to regard the grammar of colour concepts as compendiously encapsulated in the colour octahedron (and the colour wheel when black and white are not at issue). He had not canvassed the view in 'Some Remarks on Logical Form' or earlier writings, and it is to be expected that he would emphasize that the logical structure of colour is captured by this representation. Nor had he previously addressed the twin logical questions of why reddish blue is possible, reddish green impossible, and why red, blue, green and yellow count as primaries, orange and purple as mixed colours, questions he took the colour octahedron and colour wheel construed as grammar to answer.

In the 1930 lectures Wittgenstein also notes that the four primaries – red, yellow, green and blue – differ from other saturated colours with regard to 'betweenness'. The sense in which purple is between red and blue is, he stresses, different from the sense in which red is between orange and purple (Moore 1993: 108; also PR §§221–223 and MWL: 27). This is somewhat clearer for the colour octahedron, the four colours being at the corners of a square, than for the colour wheel, where the colours have no specifically demarcated positions (MWL: 26). However, while the colour octahedron is the better representation in this regard, it is still not entirely satisfactory. As Wittgenstein reportedly said: 'There is no middle point between red and blue (cf. points with no metric in geometry) and if the diagram [i.e. the base of the octahedron] suggests this, it is still misleading' (LWL: 11–12). In short, 'between' and 'midway' do not apply to colours in the way they apply to space and time. (Moore (1993: 108–109) notes that Wittgenstein 'only seem[s] to be making … assertions', that is, seems to be stating facts about colour rather than treating the logic of colour concepts.)

Wittgenstein takes 'primary colour' and 'colour', as he takes 'colour' in the *Tractatus* (4.1272), to be formal or pseudo-concepts. He holds that 'colour' marks out a category no less than 'number', 'space' and 'time', and he apparently said: 'It is nonsense to say "Red is a colour"' (LWL: 12; also compare MWL: 28: '"Red is a mixture of orange & purple" is nonsense'). His point is not that 'Red is a colour' (respectively 'Red is a mixture of orange & purple') is comparable to 'This circle is square' and '10 is a multiple of 3' but comparable rather to '1 is a number' and 'Pawns in chess only move one square at a time'. He means such sentences are empty, without significant content (and factually uninformative). Rather they are integral to our system of representation, something that cannot be represented, only presented, displayed. The difference between 'Red is a colour' and 'The book is red' is that the former rules out predicating the colour to sounds, etc., the latter that the book is a colour other than red. As Wittgenstein is described as having put it: '"Primary colour" instead of drawing a boundary within language, draws a boundary of language' (MWL: 27; also compare LWL:12: 'The pseudo-concept (colour) draws a boundary *of* language, the concept proper (red) draws a boundary *in* language'). Wittgenstein never fails to distinguish how we talk and think about things from describing how they are. For him, 'what we are doing is giving the grammatical rules and conventions applying to colour, etc' (LWL:12).

No other philosopher insists on treating colour in mathematical terms as stoutly as Wittgenstein. (Only Schopenhauer, arguably, comes close.) While he does not broadcast the fact particularly loudly in the 1930 lectures, he takes the grammar of colour to parallel the grammar of arithmetic and holds the concept of a reddish green surface is as nonsensical as the concept of a multiple of 10 not divisible by 5. For him the parallel goes pretty much without saying and to suppose otherwise is to construe language wrongly or non-standardly. Thus he maintains that perspicuous representations of colour and arithmetic (and geometry) encapsulate rules of language and an examination of either one clarifies the other. The colour octahedron and Euclidean geometry are, he notes, both 'part of grammar', each 'a convention of expression' (MWL: 18; LWL: 8) and a sentence like 'This is red' 'presupposes the colour-space' (LWL: 8; also LWL: 116). (In addition compare PR §221: 'Of course you can also arrange all the shades [of colour] in a straight line, say with black and white as endpoints, as has been done, but then you have to introduce rules to exclude certain transitions, and in the end the representation on the line must be given the same topological structure as the octahedron has'.)

'We're not at the mercy of the wheel'

After compiling *Philosophical Remarks*, Wittgenstein set about restating and reordering his thoughts with an eye to eventual publication as a book. In the resulting document, now known as *The Big Typescript* (1933–1934), he covers a wide range of subjects including colour. The volume, comprising some 140 substantial sections, supplements *Philosophical Remarks* and the 1930–1932 lectures, with remarks echoing, sometimes repeating practically word for word, earlier remarks or comments. Wittgenstein again distinguishes between logical and empirical questions, notes that he is concerned with grammar, refers to colour space, takes the colour octahedron to display relationships among colour concepts and stresses that the difference between primaries and other colours is a convention of use, not a factual truth. For instance he writes in §94 on 'Phenomenology and Grammar': 'Colour space is *roughly* represented by an octahedron, ... and this representation is grammatical. ... To say that under such and such circumstances – say – a red after-image appears, *is* psychological (*it* may or not occur, the other is *a priori*; the one can be ascertained through experiments, the other can't)' (BT: 322).

    §100 of *The Big Typescript*, 'Colour and Colour Mixing [*Farben und Farbenmischung*]' (BT, pp. 340–345), is the most sustained treatment of colour in the book (compare PR, Chapter VIII, and MS 112: 125v-134r, material drafted on 26 November 1931). Wittgenstein begins by revisiting the problem of explaining colour incompatibility. Doubtless mindful of the argument of the final paragraph of 6.3751 of the *Tractatus*, he chastises himself for thinking when he 'wrote the *Tractatus* (and later as well)' that a proposition like 'A is red' could be analysed into 'the logical product of some other proposition and ["A is not blue"]' (BT: 340; here he again stresses that he is concerned with '"colour", not "pigment"'). This was, he now concedes, a mistake, his present view being that 'this doesn't give us the proper grammar' and it is unlikely anything else will (BT: 341). Thus, tallying up, he writes: 'We've simply come to understand that we are dealing with rulers and not with isolated graduation marks, as it were. Of course the proposition 'There is only room for *one* colour in one location at one time' is a disguised grammatical proposition. Its negation isn't a contradiction [of the form 'p and not-p'], but it *contradicts* a rule of our normal grammar'.

In addition to discussing the problem of colour incompatibility, Wittgenstein says more in the first half of §100 of *The Big Typescript* about pure colours and the colour wheel. He writes: 'What we call "an intermediate colour between blue and red (or bluish red) is so called because of a relationship that shows in the grammar of the words "blue", "red" and "bluish red". . . . The relationship of pure colours to their intermediate colour[s] is of an *elementary* kind' (BT: 342; for 'elementary', perhaps read 'basic'). Moreover he notes that 'one can speak of a pure blue, yellow, green, white, black, but not of a pure orange, grey or reddish-blue'. This is not to deny that 'one *can* talk of a pure grey, in so far as one means by this a non-greenish, non-yellowish, whitish-black; and something similar holds for "pure orange", etc'. In addition he suggests that the colour circle is taken to have 'four special points' because one orange can be sensibly said to be closer to red than a second one. As always Wittgenstein is concerned with the grammar of colour concepts and logical relationships among individual colours. He is, he says, speaking of colours 'not on the plane of the colour circle, but within *colour space* [*nicht in der Ebene des Farbenkreises, sondern im* Farbenraum]'.

The importance Wittgenstein attaches to colour space is also apparent in a remark on the colour top (*Farbenkreisel*), a device that mixes colours when spun. He notes that he is talking about the mixtures of colours produced by the colour top properly understood and would have it noticed that 'the colour wheel produces the mixture only in so far as we can perceive it as a mixture', that is, only insofar as we can see a wheel that is half red and half yellow turning orange as it is spun (BT: 342). 'We're not at the mercy of the wheel', and were a whitish colour to result when a half red, half yellow wheel is spun, we would no more say 'the immediate colour between red and yellow was whitish orange' than we would say '3 + 4 is 6 if, when putting 3 and 4 apples together one was to disappear'. 'The colour wheel [is used] not as an experiment but for a calculation'; that is, it is comparable to a mathematical proof (BT: 343). (Compare TLP 6.2331: 'Calculation is not an experiment'. Also Z §347.) 'The transition from colour to colour on the colour wheel [is different from the] transition that we encounter when we see little patches of the one colour mixed in with little patches of the other one.' The relation of 'between' in the two cases 'doesn't coincide'. One is physical, the other grammatical.

Besides the remarks already mentioned, Wittgenstein has a number of other remarks of interest in *The Big Typescript*. He notes various additional facts about our use of colour language, raises questions about how it is properly understood and touches on his own earlier discussion of the topic. Thus he points out that 'A' in 'A is yellow' has one grammar when it picks out a body, another one when it picks out the surface of an object (BT: 28), observes that some colours, grey would be one, are in 'the space of darker and lighter' (BT: 85) and reminds us that 'primary colour' is categorically different from 'moon of Jupiter' since 'grammar can't be justified by reality' (BT: 148). In addition he declares 'it is nonsense to say . . . the rules for the words "blue" and "red" agree with the facts about those colours, etc' (BT: 232), asks: 'Does the word "colour" . . . have a different meaning when it refers to shapes close to the edge [of visual space]?' (BT: 337), wonders what reason could be cited for counting something 'a colour if it does not fit in with the colour scheme we have been using so far' (BT: 369) and compares '4 primary colours' with '7 notes in an octave' (BT: 421). Also he admits (BT: 249) that he erred in the *Tractatus* because he failed to distinguish between 'All the primary colours can be found in this picture', primary colours being listable, and 'All people die before they are 200', people not being similarly listable.

'The only difference being in the jingle of the words'

After completing the 1933 version of *The Big Typescript* Wittgenstein shifted direction and began attending more closely to topics related to private experience. During the 1933/1934 academic year he dictated to a small group of students a set of remarks subsequently published as *The Blue Book*, a number of copies of which were made and circulated, including one he dispatched to Russell to inform him about his latest thinking, something he had promised to do. In contrast to earlier work which focused on the representation of space, time, colour, etc., *The Blue Book* focuses on 'words which describe what are called "mental activities": seeing, hearing, feeling, etc' (BBB: 70). Wittgenstein mainly mentions colour to bolster general philosophical points rather than to illuminate the ins-and-outs of colour language. For instance he could have explored why a person, instructed to paint a red patch, paints a red one by considering why someone, instructed to draw a straight line, draws one (BBB: 15). It is not true, however, that there is nothing more on colour language (and the logic of colour concepts) as such until *Remarks on Colour* of 1950. From time to time Wittgenstein returns to the question of the logical character of colour, sometimes in familiar ways, sometimes in markedly new ways.

Wittgenstein takes the complexity of the concept of 'same' to be underappreciated, and in *The Blue Book*, he discusses the concept of 'same colour' in some detail. We are not, he notes, forced to acknowledge that two books have the same colour, it being also reasonable to say 'they can't have the *same* colour, because, after all, this book has its colour, and the other book has its own colour too' (BBB: 55). Neither way of talking is cast in stone. They are just different ways of talking, the appropriateness of which depends on the circumstances and what the speaker means to convey. In addition Wittgenstein warns against supposing colours cannot occur together because they are 'in each other's way' (BBB: 56). It is, he observes, one thing to say: 'Two colours occur at the same place at the same time', another to say: 'Three people cannot sit side by side on a bench'. (Arguably, the difference is sloughed over in RLF: 34.) While the proposition about persons on a bench records 'a physical impossibility', the proposition about colours occurring together records a logical or mathematical impossibility (BBB: 56). The proposition 'sounds English' and 'there are closely similar forms of expression ... in other departments of our language' but it is in fact 'somewhat analogous to saying: "3 x 18 inches won't go into 3 feet"'.

In *The Yellow Book*, a record of informal discussions contemporaneous with *The Blue Book*, 'This is green and yellow at the same time' is said to be no less nonsensical than 'Ab sur ab', 'the only difference being in the jingle of the words' (AWL: 64). It is a common error, Wittgenstein observes, to think there is 'nonsense which makes sense and nonsense which does not'. His point is not that 'This is green and yellow at the same time' is grammatically out of order and cannot be of use (e.g. when teaching language). He is not saying the sentence is mere noise and retracting his view that 'No two colours can jointly occur' is a rule, not a description. To the contrary, he more naturally and charitably read as noting that the sentence does not convey information. And he would have us agree too that 'in our grammar of colour it makes no sense to talk of a seventh primary colour since we have only six primary-colour words' ('red', 'blue', 'green', 'yellow', 'white' and 'black') and 'the expression "primary colour number seven" has no meaning' (AWL: 66). 'There is no parallelism between "There is no seventh primary colour" and "There is no 6'2" man who can be fitted with the six sizes of suits manufactured'". Moreover it is useless to hold the notion of a seventh primary is senseless because 'the grammar of "colour" is arbitrary'. 'What it would be reasonable to ask is whether there would be any use for "seventh primary colour"'.

Like *The Blue Book, The Brown Book* (1934/1935) was dictated to students. While Wittgenstein focuses in this work on how language is acquired, he has occasion to point out that 'we use the word "similar" in a huge family of cases' (BBB: 133). 'In certain cases', he notes, 'we should say [a bluish green and a greenish yellow] are similar and in others that they are most dissimilar'. To say light blue and dark blue are similar because they have blue in common 'is really a tautology', an empty grammatical remark rather than an empirical truth, and were someone to ask what light and dark blue have in common, 'the answer . . . really ought to be "I don't know what game you are playing"' (BBB: 134). Imagine someone, ordered to divide a pile of slightly reddish brown and slightly greenish yellow leaves into red and green piles, separating the reddish-brown ones from the greenish yellow ones (see BBB: 137). Should we say the person is using 'red' and 'green' the usual way or differently? 'One might say "red" means something different in the two cases' but then again 'why shouldn't [one] say that it had one meaning only but was, of course, used according to the circumstances?' Which use is apt depends on the context of utterance and 'the natural reactions of the people using the language' (BBB: 138).

When Wittgenstein was compiling *The Brown Book*, his newfound interest in the acquisition of language and understanding was firmly in place but his long-standing interest in representation and the logic of colour concepts was not left completely behind. Thus in the earliest version of the *Philosophical Investigations* (1936–37), the *Urfassung*, he not only discusses ostensive teaching (and the definition) of colour words at some length (PU/UF §29, PI §30), he also questions whether 'red' names something utterly lacking in complexity (§44/§47) and suggests that were a sample of sepia 'preserved in Paris like the standard metre', it would 'make no sense to state of this sample either that it is of this colour or that it is not' (§49/§50). Moreover he challenges various commonly held views about colour. In particular he takes issue with the claim that red is indestructible (§55/§57) and the claim that 'one cannot say "Red exists", because if there were no red, it could not be spoken of at all' (§56/§58). And – echoing his remarks about light and dark blue – he declares that 'phenomena [of language] have no one thing in common in virtue of which we use the same word for all', there being no essential features, only similarities and differences, even of colours (§62/§65; also §§69–70/§§72–73; for more on this material see Lugg 2000).

'Exactly so . . .. We are calculating with these colour terms'

Wittgenstein regularly compared colour concepts with mathematical concepts and took conceptual truths about colours to be relevantly similar to mathematical truths. Time and again he treated impossible colour concepts, notably 'reddish green', to be as aberrant as impossible arithmetical concepts such as 'even prime number greater than 2', refers to the likes of 'White is darker than black' and the likes of '1 + 1 = 3' as both contradictory, and insists that our criteria for combining colours (not pigments) and our criteria for adding numbers (not groups of objects) are logical, not empirical. (There would, he repeatedly noted, be something unusual happening if mixing red and yellow resulted in blue no less than there would be something happening if adding two apples to two apples resulted in three apples.) Few differences are more important to Wittgenstein's way of thinking than the difference between what he variously calls logical, conceptual and mathematical truth and what he variously calls empirical, factual and experiential truth. It is, he insists, essential that the two kinds of concept, proposition and criterion be separated, and when discussing colours and numbers, he harps on the difference. Nobody should find it surprising that colour is discussed in *Remarks on the Foundations of Mathematics* (1937–1944) and *Lectures on the Foundations of Mathematics* (1939).

In Part I of RFM (probably 1937–1938), Wittgenstein notes – it is practically a stock example of his – that 'White is lighter than black' is 'non-temporal' and expresses 'an *internal* relation' (I.104). (Compare this proposition with 'This patch is darker than that one', a temporal proposition expressing an external relation.) The statement about white and black is, he stresses, akin to 'a machine on paper' (I.102). It 'does not express the result of an experiment' and is 'not subject to wind and weather like physical things' (I.103). To the contrary, a 'picture of a black and a white patch serves us *simultaneously* as a paradigm of what we understand by "lighter" and "darker" and as a paradigm for "white" and for "black"' (I.105). 'Our proposition is non-temporal because it only expresses the connection of the words "white", "black" and "lighter" with a paradigm'. For Wittgenstein – it is central to his thinking – the connection between words and things, be they colour words or numerals, is 'set up in language'. (It is no accident that I.102–105 is sandwiched between remarks about numbers and geometrical propositions. Also see I.155 where judging a colour differently at different times is compared with finding a calculation acceptable at one time and unacceptable later.)

In *Lectures on the Foundations of Mathematics*, Wittgenstein returns to the topic of colour incompatibility when discussing 'the notion that the laws of logic are laws of thought' and the fact that 'p and not-p' is never true (LFM:

231). 'Propositions regarded as synthetic *a priori* like "A patch cannot be at the same time both red and green"' are, he argues, like the law of contradiction in that they 'show what we *do* with propositions, as opposed to expressing opinions or convictions' (LFL: 232). True, but there is more to be said. The claim that a patch '*can't* be both red and yellow in the same way it *can* be both red and oblong' leaves unaddressed the question: 'What does "in the same way" mean?' (The issue being raised coincides with the issue Wittgenstein later discusses under the rubric of following a rule.) We are supposed to notice that what 'we do' with colour propositions is subject to choice, not fixed in advance. 'Red and yellow at the same place at the same time' can be accorded a meaning despite conflicting with prevailing linguistic practice. Nothing would go wrong if we accepted such an incompatibility. It would only 'upset our system', which 'means simply upsetting *us*' (LFM: 235). 'It would come to building a system that would be decidedly impractical'. (Compare building a number system of numbers without zero or for some applications complex numbers.)

We are no more ready 'to continue the series': red and soft, red and oblong, red and blue, with 'red and green', than we are ready to continue the series: square, triangle, biangle, with 'monangle' (LFM: 233; if 'red and blue' is taken to refer to two colours rather than purple, we shall stop there, and likewise if 'biangle' is taken to refer to a line rather than a plane figure). 'There is no reddish green' is 'as different as hell' from 'In this room there is nothing yellowish-green' (LFM: 243). (The 'reality' that 'There is no reddish green' is supposed to correspond to is 'entirely parallel to Hardy's "reality"', that is, the reality that the Cambridge mathematician G.H. Hardy believed mathematical propositions are responsible to.) Moreover were 'a colour mixer top' to produce black 'when it was spun with red and yellow discs', you would not be 'inclined to say black is a blend of red and yellow' for 'experience [is not] our criterion' (LFM: 234). As the famous mathematician Alan Turing, present at the lectures, reportedly interjected, 'mixture' is being used like 'multiply'. To which Wittgenstein, predictably given the line he is pioneering, is said to have replied: 'Exactly so. That is just what I am driving at. We are *calculating* with these colour terms.'

It bears underlining that Wittgenstein casts the logic of colour concepts in calculus-like terms rather than language-game terms. When discussing it, he no more zeroes in on the role language plays in our lives than he does when he discussing arithmetic. Actually he does the opposite. He refers to language-games when focusing on features of language connected with use, calculi when focusing on its 'calculating' features. Not unreasonably he takes colour language and arithmetic to comprise systematically interrelated terms, red, blue, green, yellow, etc., in the one case, 0, 1, 2, 3, etc., in the other, and would have deemed it misleading to invoke language-games to explain such interrelation-ships. When discussing the logic of arithmetic, he does not mention the habits and behaviour of mathematicians (nor, incidentally, does Russell in his discussion of mathematics), and when discussing the logic of colour concepts, he does not mention the habits and behaviour of users of colour language. In this regard it should be remembered that Wittgenstein says in the *Investigations* (PI §7) that 'a language-game' comprises two things, not one: 'language and the activities into which it is woven'.

Other Discussions and Further Reading

Not all the notes recorded in LWL reappear in MWL. When both are available, Moore's more detailed notes are accorded priority. For the initial composition of the *Big Typescript* and its subsequent revision, see the 'Editors' Introduction' (BT: vi–vii, ix). The remarks Wittgenstein drafted in the 1930s and 1940s are closely examined in Hilmy 1987, Paul 2007, Engelmann 2013 and the essays in Figueiredo 2023, while the more specific remarks on colour drafted during the period are discussed in the essays in Gierlinger & Riegelnik 2014 and Silva 2017. It is not true (Blank 2008: 312) that 'after assembling the *Big Typescript* [in 1932/ 33], Wittgenstein put aside the issues connected with colour, only to take them up again in comparable detail almost twenty years later, in the *Remarks on Colour* (1950)'. It is often maintained that Wittgenstein traded 'the calculus model of language' in the mid-1930s for 'the language-game model' (see, e.g., Hacker 1986: 132). Also compare Stern (2018), Pichler (2018) and Dehnel (2023: 1–4) for helpful discussion. For the view that Wittgenstein continues to use calculus-related terminology in the late 1930s and subsequently, see Hilmy 1987: 98 and Lugg 2013. When it came to the representation (and logic) of colour concepts, Wittgenstein's interest did not shift 'from the "geometry" of a symbolism (whether a language or a calculus) to its place in human life, its use in human behaviour and discourse' (Hacker 1986: 132).

4 Wittgenstein on Colour, 1940–1949

'Essentially . . . still the same' or 'completely different'

In 1940 and 1941 Wittgenstein continued to explore themes associated with the early version of the *Investigations* and to work on the philosophy of mathematics with an occasional glance at the logic of colour concepts. Later, between November 1941 and February 1944, he was involved in the war effort, working first as an orderly at Guy's Hospital in London, then as an assistant in a medical research unit in Newcastle. While at Guy's, however, he met students on Saturday evenings and continued his philosophical work, work that resulted in three notebooks and a manuscript volume, again with more than a few references of significance to colour. Only in March 1944, when staying with Rush Rhees, then teaching in Swansea, did he once more devote himself fully to philosophy. During these years he had occasion to compare propositions about colours with propositions about numbers, to speak of the geometry of colour, to take the impossibility of reddish green to be akin to a mathematical impossibility, to refer to the gap between red and green as 'geometrical' and to note that the structure of colour rules out reddish green (compare the impossibility of a one-inch square peg fitting into a round hole one inch in diameter).

In a remark drafted in 1940 Wittgenstein imagines the possibility of referring to the colour of an object by referring to what it is not. In this event, he notes, 'where I see *blue* this means the object that I see is *not* blue' (RFM, III.80). 'I should like to shew', he explains, 'that we could be led to want to describe something's being blue, both by saying it is blue, and by saying it is not blue', his reason being, presumably, that this would show colour words are linked to colours only through the intercession of linguistic custom. Later, in 1942, he will couple the question of whether experience reveals that different colours cannot occur at the same place with the question of whether experience reveals that a straight line is possible between any two points (IV.4). He allows there is 'a germ of truth' in the suggestion that '*imagination* tells us' what can and cannot occur but thinks the suggestion is easily misunderstood. While acknowledging that experience may help us see that two colours cannot occur in the same place, he insists that the proposition that they cannot so occur 'does not play the part of an empirical proposition'. Also in 1942 he points out that a white that turns black – at, say, dusk – may be regarded as 'essentially … still the same' or '*completely* different' (IV.38). Judgements of colour vary and people differ on the question of when they are the same and when not.

On 13 August 1941 Wittgenstein apparently noted in discussion with the psychologist Robert Thouless, a Cambridge acquaintance, that given 'a transparent cube which looked red from one side and green from the other', one might say: 'Here we see red and green at the same place at the same time' (WWT: 387). Perhaps, but this is far from colour incompatibility, the crucial claim of which is 'red and green can't be at the same place at the same time in the way that red and soft can' (WWT: 388). As in his 1939 lectures on mathematics, Wittgenstein holds it is senseless to speak of 'pass[ing] analogically from red and soft to red and green'. The snag is that it is, as often the case with analogies, unclear what counts as analogous. It is not even determined what comes after 1, 2, 3, …, 1000, and it is neither here nor there that 'all people would make the same decision'. This only encourages 'the mystical idea that we understand [the formula governing the series] intuitively'. Also, Thouless reports Wittgenstein as having declared that propositions like 'Black is darker than white' are timeless 'grammatical proposition[s]' not significantly different from 'propositions of mathematics'. (In 1942, again associating colour with mathematics, Wittgenstein refers to the 'colour-geometrical observations' encapsulated in the colour circle (MS 126: 29–30).)

Several other remarks about colour reproduced in *Remarks on the Foundations* anticipate themes in the *Investigations* and *On Certainty* (PI: 240–242; OC: 105ff; also 281 and 674). In 1943 or 1944, if not earlier, Wittgenstein wrote: 'It is of the greatest importance that a dispute hardly ever arises between people about whether the colour of this object is the same as the colour of that' (VI.21) and states that 'the certainty with which I call [a] colour "red" is the rigidity of my measuring-rod', though 'of course … a slip of the tongue' is always possible (VI.28). If people 'did not agree with me [that the green colour I am seeing is called "green"]', he announces, 'I should become totally confused and should perhaps take them or myself for crazy' (VI.35). It is, after all, 'of the greatest importance that all or the enormous majority of us agree in certain things' and we can be 'quite sure' that green will be 'called "green" by far the most of the human beings who see it' (VI.39). This is not an a priori truth but rather an acknowledgement of the fact that without agreement there would be turmoil. Moreover, in a remark dated 15 March 1944 on our agreement on the basic colours, Wittgenstein asks: 'What right have I to say: "Yes, that's red"?' and replies: 'Well, I say it; and it cannot be justified. And it is characteristic of this language-game … that all men consent to it without question' (VII.40).

In the summer of 1944 Wittgenstein decided to supplement the *Urfassung* with remarks about psychological concepts rather than remarks about mathematics, a decision that led in the fullness of time to *Philosophical Investigations*, his second great book. While colour is not entirely absent from this work, it is mostly referred to, naturally enough, in the context of a discussion of our mental lives and our behaviour ('the inner' and 'the outer'). As usual, Wittgenstein proceeds from topic to topic and provides what he refers to as 'sketches of landscapes' (Preface, ix). He is, however, plausibly regarded as directing his (mostly scattered) remarks on colour against the view, commonly embraced by non-philosophers and philosophers alike, that our colour concepts are correct and our system of colours mirrors essential facts about colour. Thus he again challenges the connection that many philosophers see between colour words and images (§239), and in the course of examining the concept of a logically private language he disputes the suggestion that 'we at least *mean* something quite definite when we look at a colour and name our colour impression' (§276). 'It is', he declares, 'virtually as if we detached the colour *impression* from the object', a practice that 'ought to arouse our suspicions.'

'"Natural", not "necessary"'

After compiling the final version of *Philosophical Investigations*, Wittgenstein wrote a substantial amount on psychological concepts subsequently published under the title *Remarks on the Philosophy of Psychology*. Continuing to reflect on our system of colour concepts, he says: 'It is interesting . . . to observe that particular shapes are not tied to particular colours in our environment. . . . If we imagined a world in which shapes and colours *were* always tied to one another . . . we'd find intelligible a system of concepts, in which the fundamental division – shape and colour – did not hold' (RPP I.47). Similarly we might, he adds, proceed differently were primary colours encountered only rarely and in connection with other colours. If, for instance, red was seen just when the tips of leaves changed from green to red in the autumn, 'nothing would be more natural than to call red a degenerate green'. This is not to suggest our system of concepts encapsulates truths, only to acknowledge that were 'the facts of nature . . . different we should have different concepts' (RPP 1.48). 'If you believe our concepts are the right ones', Wittgenstein would have you 'imagine certain general facts of nature different from the way they are'. Conjure up such facts and 'conceptual structures different from our own will', he states, 'appear *natural* to you'. That is, he immediately adds, '"natural", not "necessary"' (RPP I.49). (Also compare RPP I.626 on red as 'the ultimate degeneration of green'.)

In another series of remarks in the same volume Wittgenstein ponders the suggestion that 'red' – and more generally 'colour' – is inexplicable (RPP I.602–604, Z §§368–369). He writes: 'Quite right: one can't imagine any explanation of "red" or of "colour". Not, however, because what is experienced is something specific, but rather because the language-game is so', that is, how we happen to proceed (RPP I.602). 'Red' is inexplicable because the colour red is a basic element in our scheme of concepts, not because it is (metaphysically) fundamental and absolutely simple. It is after all conceivable that another people use a complicated 'kind of binary decimal fraction', for example, 'R, LLRL', to indicate that 'yellow stands to the right, and red to the left' (RPP I.603). The difference between R,LLRL-users and us is like the difference between people with a special talent and the rest of us. As Wittgenstein puts it: 'They [R,LLRL-users] would stand to us roughly in the relation of people with absolute pitch to people in whom this is wanting. *They can do* what we can't.' It is tempting to query whether this is 'even imaginable', that is, a person could have such a 'colour experience' (RPP I.604). In response Wittgenstein says it is difficult to know what to answer. Would we think, before 'encounter-[ing] people with absolute pitch', that 'the existence of such people [is] very probable'?

Nor is there much to be said for the philosophical claim that red is simple, 'not composite' (RPP I.605, Z §338). This is unlike 'This chair is composite', a context for which is easily imagined (imagine noting its seat, arms and legs are made of different pieces). The fact that it is hard to know, in the normal course of events, what someone saying 'Red is composite' could mean is, Wittgenstein observes, 'an *important* fact', though what 'kind of fact' is difficult to say. The trouble is that 'we are not familiar with any technique to which the sentence might be alluding'; that is, we have no idea how the sentence might be used. There is no describing 'a language-game that we *cannot learn*' (RPP I.606), and no reason to think this shows something different is going on behind the scenes, 'something that we are not acquainted with', as opposed to merely showing 'what we *go by* in judging of inner processes' (§607). The difficulty of describing what occurs in people is no indication of something special going on in their minds, that their 'inner process' is different. (Compare §644, Z §332: 'Don't believe you have the concept of colour within you because however you look, you look upon a coloured object.' This is like thinking 'you have the concept of a negative number because you are in debt'.)

It is no good objecting that we know what red is since we can 'point to something red', more being required to pin down the statement 'That is red' than an 'ostensive definition' (RPP I.608). There is a huge difference between pointing to red objects and pointing to the colour red, and no possibility of ruling out ahead of time that 'red' is not 'the name of a shape' (I.613; also compare PI §28 and the accompanying note). Still it is 'important' that '"red" does not get explained to anyone without reference to a sample of the colour' (RPP I.609). Red (or redness) is not 'a particular sense-impression, known only to him who has it (or has had it)' and wrong to suppose there is no explaining what 'red' means apart from '*producing* [the sense-impression] in the other person' (I.610). What the word means is, as a matter of fact, explicable in various ways. It might, for instance, be explained by pointing to a reddish dark brown, then to a yellow, then to a black, and finally saying the original colour contains a third colour (I.612). In Wittgenstein's eyes linguistic practice is the arbiter of linguistic meaning. 'The language-game with colours is characterised by what we are able to do, and what we are not able to do' (I.618).

Many other remarks in volume 1 of *Remarks on the Philosophy of Psychology* provide glimpses into Wittgenstein's thinking about colour concepts. He considers the supposed 'specificity' of red (RPP I.619–620, I.628–630) and the notion of a primary colour, noting in particular that 'it would be very remarkable if the equality of distances [between them on the colour circle] lay in the nature of things' (I.622–623). In addition he observes that '"There's no such thing as a reddish green" is akin to the propositions that we use as axioms in mathematics' (I.624; compare Z §346: 'Would accepting "There is such a thing as reddish green" upset the system the way accepting "2 + 2 = 5" would? Probably not but the difference is just one of degree surely'). And he states that whereas '*purple* is "blue and red', '*olive-green* [is not] "red and green"' (RPP I.857, Z §361). Also it is of interest that he discusses synaesthesia (RPP I.16, I.100, I.328, I.836), faint colours (I.219), the notion of sameness of colour (I.547), the relation of red to purple (I.641), different colour attribution (I.645) and the similarity between blending colours and blending smells, sounds and tastes (I.783). Throughout he aims to steer us away from error, misunderstanding and confusion. The exercise is critical and exploratory, not theoretical and explanatory.

'We have a colour system as we have a number system'

In the remarks published in Volume II of *Remarks on the Philosophy of Psychology* (1948). Wittgenstein again broaches the subject of how our system of colour concepts might change were the world markedly different. He first asks how it might differ were grass not green, blood not red and other colour words similarly unconnected with the colours of things (RPP II.197), then considers the possibility of teaching children the words for colours if objects were constantly changing colour (II.198), and rounds out the sequence of remarks by pondering whether colour words could be learnt were everything the same colour (II.199). None of this discredits that colour terms are, as Wittgenstein insists, logically interrelated. However dependent our system of colour concepts may be on how things are, physical or human, it is not determined by them. Also Wittgenstein envisions a world in which we are surrounded by definite shades of light blue and dark blue and conjectures that our colour concepts would be similar to but different from our present concepts (II.294–295; compare the number concepts of a people who only count to five). Moreover he canvasses the possibility of a concept corresponding to our 'red' on one side of a dividing line, our 'green' on the other side (II.398–399) and lists eight ways that 'colour might play a different role' in 'a world different from ours' (II.658). Even in the simplest of cases, he intimates, our colour words are 'arbitrary', not forced on us.

As if to forestall the mistake of thinking colour language mirrors how it is in the world, Wittgenstein writes: '"There is no such thing as bluish yellow" . . . is like "There is no such thing as a regular biangle"; this could be called a proposition of colour-geometry, i.e., it is a proposition determining a concept' (RPP II.421). Put otherwise the concept of bluish yellow is comparable to the geometrically incongruous concept of a biangle and partially serves to define the concept of colour just as the concept of a biangle partially serves to define the concept of geometrical figure; that is, 'bluish yellow' rules out the possibility of a mixture of blue and yellow in much the same way as 'biangle' rules out the possibility of a regular plain figure with just two angles. It is no good saying: 'By "bluish yellow" I mean green' since the expression, as originally intended, 'signifies a different road, a *no thoroughfare*' (II.425, Z §356). The sole remaining question of interest is whether the right simile is 'that of a road that is physically impassable, or of the non-existence of a road? i.e. is it one of physical or mathematical impossibility?' For Wittgenstein, no two ways about it, it is a mathematical / logical impossibility.

Wittgenstein takes 'reddish green' and 'bluish yellow' to be logically abnormal, and starting at RPP II.422 he comments further on their abnormality. He imagines instructing someone who had been taught 'the names of the six primary colours' (i.e. 'red', 'green', 'blue', 'yellow', 'white' and 'black') and the use of 'the suffix "ish"' to 'paint a greenish white'. Assuming the teaching is successful, the person will have no difficulty producing what is required. But imagine changing the order to 'Paint a reddish green'. It is likely that the person will 'mix green and red and not be satisfied with the result'. Neither brown nor black merges red and green in the manner reddish blue merges red and blue (and the result is not, as reddish blue sometimes is, a bright colour). Sooner or later, Wittgenstein observes, the person 'may say "There's no such thing as a reddish green"'. (Compare calling on someone to construct a biangle or give the square root of −25.) In the case of red and green, Wittgenstein writes: 'I want to say there is a *geometrical* gap, not a physical one between [them]' (RPP II.423, Z §354). 'If we teach a human being such-and-such a technique by means of examples, . . . 'this and not that [may be] the "natural" continuation for him: this of itself is an extremely important fact of nature' (RPP II.424, Z §355).

By way of summarizing the discussion, Wittgenstein writes: 'We have a colour system [*System der Farben*] as we have a number system [*System der Zahlen*]. Do the systems reside in *our* nature or the nature of things? How are we to put it? *Not* in the nature of numbers or colours' (RPP II.426, Z §357). What exactly Wittgenstein means here is not crystal clear but it can be safely said he would have us appreciate that the systems are not rooted in how we are or how things are; that is, they are not responsible to anything beyond themselves. Nor, he underlines, do they 'reside' in the concepts of number and colour themselves, that is, how we think and speak about them. Does this mean there is, he asks, 'something arbitrary about [such a] system' (RPP II.427, Z §358)? As so often, he answers: 'Yes and no'. The system is, he declares, 'akin both to what is arbitrary and what is not arbitrary' (Compare BT §56. 'The Rules of Grammar . . . are not Answerable to any Meaning and in this Respect are

Arbitrary'. Also compare RPP I.46, II.393 and II.727, Z §§351–352. Incidentally RPP II.426 and RPP II.427 are separated in MS 137: 6, the source of Volume II of RPP, by '"Bluish yellow" coincides with a hole [*fällt auf ein Loch*]'.)

To round out this series of remarks Wittgenstein looks into the possibility of a people who find the concept of reddish green perfectly intelligible and think its exclusion unreasonable. Presuming it is 'obvious' that there is no such colour as reddish green even if it takes experience and education to see it, he asks: 'What would we think of people … who called olive-green by that name?' (RPP II.428, Z §359 in part). It is futile to respond: 'They have a different concept of colour' and point to an object with another colour 'as if there were an *object* to which the colour belongs unequivocally'. As already noted, concepts cannot be identified simply by pointing to objects. But if this does not settle the matter, how is it known that 'there *is* no such thing [as reddish green]' (RPP II.429, Z §362)? It is not that a person who claims to be acquainted with reddish green is 'too stupid' to notice the discrepancy between our way and their way of talking (RPP II.431, Z §363). Perhaps recalling what he said at RPP II.426 about our systems of numbers and colours not residing in our nature or the nature of things, Wittgenstein agrees that nature has something 'to say here' but thinks that 'she makes herself audible in another way', there being no guarantee that we would have ended up with our system of colour concepts were nature significantly different (RPP II.432, Z §364). Finally, elaborating on RPP II.424, Wittgenstein adjudges it 'an extremely important fact that … we are not able to recognize straight off a colour that has come about by mixing red and green' but, true to form, he promptly adds within parentheses (to indicate there is still more to be said): 'But what does "straight off" signify here?' (RPP II.433, Z §365).

'They wouldn't be using our concept of colour'

The two volumes of *Last Writings on the Philosophy of Psychology* (1948–1951) cover much the same ground as the two volumes of *Remarks on the Philosophy of Psychology* (1946–1948). (Had the source of LW I been a typescript rather than a pair of manuscripts, it might have been published as RPP III. LW II overlaps with *Remarks on Colour* and includes no more than a few incidental remarks on colour concepts.) In LW I, as in RPP I and RPP II, Wittgenstein mentions facts about our use of language that he thinks should be kept in mind when reflecting on colour, challenges questionable views about language that we are apt to take for granted, and draws attention to problems about language that we are likely, if at all philosophically minded, to find puzzling. He again observes that we are mostly in agreement about the use of basic colour words, 'red', 'blue', 'green', etc., and too quick to take red and a host of other colours to be (metaphysically) simple. Moreover while convinced that the likes of bluish yellow and reddish green are logically, not merely physically, impossible, he is troubled by the thought that a tribe might possess a system of colours different from our own, this being both reasonably credited and reasonably doubted.

In Volume II of *Remarks on the Philosophy of Psychology* Wittgenstein suggested our colour concepts might function differently were the world substantially different (II.658), and in Volume I of *Last Writings on the Philosophy of Psychology*, he takes issue with the suggestion that people who 'differed strongly in their statements about colour . . . couldn't use our concept of colour', the truth of the matter being rather that they 'wouldn't be using *our concept of colour*' (I.42). In addition he wonders 'what consequences would seem plausible to us' were colours 'to play a different role in the human world than they now do' (I.207). But rather than look into the matter, he asks, 'what sort of colour concepts – different from ours – wouldn't seem odd' and invites us to 'consider various cases' (I.208), those listed in Volume II of RPP, presumably, included. Still dissatisfied with this way of rephrasing the question, however, he again notes that we are disinclined to think there are systems of concepts other than our own. 'It is', he adds, 'very it hard to imagine concepts other than our own because we never become aware of certain general facts of nature' (LW I.209). (Compare the warning in RPP (I §48) against taking our concepts to be 'the right ones, the ones suited to intelligent human beings'.) We are, Wittgenstein thinks, prone to regard empirical facts as permanently fixed and to forget that we might, for instance, only see the world in shades of grey (compare RPP II.658).

Wittgenstein also dwells more in Volume I of *Last Writings* on the intricacies of colour language. He notes that while typically reckoned 'a colour combination', brown is not taken to be one of the six colours normally regarded as pure (I.213), questions the commonly held view that '*light* is white' (I.214), stresses that 'we have a concept of colour blending which supersedes all physical methods of blending colours' (I.215) and observes that 'we judge whether according to our concept . . . two colours . . . really *should* produce [a third] colour' (I.216). Moreover he points out that how we come by a concept is 'really irrelevant' (I.217) and suggests that were conditions very different we might 'perceive all colours as combinations of white and black', it being conceivable that 'white and black pigments produced red, green' (I.219). Furthermore he observes that were there 'only *one* shade of red and green' we might take 'red and green [to be] the same', it being possible that 'in nature [red and green] always blend into each other (as certain leaves do in autumn)' (I.220), and he remarks that it could happen that 'the difference between red and green isn't *important* to [a people] as it is to us (I.221; compare I.212 on the possibility of a person 'count[ing] only on his fingers', not as 'a method of counting, but [as] counting [itself]').

Also in Volume I of *Last Writings* Wittgenstein conjectures that a person who 'associated one colour with a, e, i and another to o and u . . . would differ from us to a far greater extent than those who associated no colours at all to the vowels' (I.362–363), asks: 'Does [a person who reported he saw a colour he couldn't describe] have to be expressing himself correctly, [even] mean a colour' (I.403) and, revisiting another old worry, wonders whether 'it make[s] sense to say that people generally agree in their judgements of colour?' (I.930). If they did not generally agree, should we regard their colour words as meaning the same as ours? 'We can', Wittgenstein avers, 'say the one thing or the other. . . . There are reasons for still calling [them] the same, as well as reasons not to'. This in turn prompts him ask: 'But what about this: "Generally people don't argue about their colour judgements"? . . . Isn't that a sentence about the *concept* of colour judgement?' (I.931). To which he responds: 'If there were no agreement in 'colour-judgements, how would human beings even learn to use the words for colours? (I.932). In Volume II of *Last Writings* he questions whether the 'other colour concepts' people might possess are actually 'colour concepts' (II: 44) and states, presumably as a reminder, that leaves changing from green to red are commonly said to be reddish-green (II: 59).

More can be said about the ideas about colour that Wittgenstein expresses in remarks composed in the 1940s. But, hopefully, enough has been said to indicate how he proceeds (and the kind of investigation of colour concepts he takes himself to be undertaking). In these remarks – also the remarks penned in the 1930s and arguably earlier – he zeroes in on specific features of colour language and the assumption of philosophers of old (and many recent philosophers) that the phenomenon itself is of particular interest and consequence. He tackles the problems he critically examines one at a time in the 'piecemeal' manner extolled by Russell (1917: Chapter VI). (Arguably, Wittgenstein treats problems more resolutely piecemeal than Russell and looks far less kindly on the possibility of an overarching philosophical theory.) In the 1930s and 1940s, when it comes to colour, he isolates and clarifies how colour language is used and is as eager to pinpoint new philosophical problems as to solve old ones. It is hard to read him as doing anything other than illuminating the use of colour language and attending to traps it sets for the unwary. As he summarized his view of the business near the end of life: 'The philosopher wants to master the geography of concepts' (MS 137: 63a, dated 1 July 1948).

Other Discussions and Further Reading

For more on the composition of the material reproduced in *Remarks on the Foundations of Mathematics*, see Nedo 1993: 40–44 and Floyd 2022: 104–107 as well as von Wright 1993: 502. For Wittgenstein's thinking in 1941 both in general and regarding colour see WWT, an understudied series of conversations between Wittgenstein and R.H. Thouless (and occasionally C.H. Waddington) in which Wittgenstein touches on many topics he stresses elsewhere. For instance Thouless records him as saying: 'Black is darker than white is a proposition like the propositions of mathematics. These too are timeless' (WWT: 388). On *Remarks on the Philosophy of Psychology*, volumes I and II, and *Last Writings on the Philosophy of Psychology*, volumes I and II, see Schulte 2016 and Trächtler 2022: 108–112 as well as von Wright 1993: 503. For discussion of Wittgenstein's statement that '*We have a colour system as we have a number system*' see Schulte 2014. The thoughts expressed at RPP I.47–49 about the possibility of different systems of colour concepts are reiterated in PPF, section xii (§§365–366).

5 Wittgenstein on Colour, 1950: New Thoughts

'I read a great deal in Goethe's "Farbenlehre"'

Wittgenstein's treatment of colour in *Remarks on Colour* (1950) is by far his most sustained treatment of the topic. Much less apparent is why he would devote so much time and effort exploring the ins-and-outs of colour language at this stage of his life. He was not gathering together and reordering remarks on the subject he had composed during the last two decades. As G.E.M. Anscombe says in her 'Editor's Preface', the material 'gives a clear sample of first-draft writing and subsequent selection'. Nor is he credibly regarded as having turned his attention to colour because he was going through a lean patch and keen to spark a thought or two. He was at the time hard at work on the relationship between our 'inner' mental life and our 'outer' behaviour. Far more likely, surely, he took up the topic because he noticed something, a fact or puzzle, about the logic of colour concepts that had eluded his attention, something he felt he needed to discuss. He was not in the habit of returning to an issue unless he expected to discover something new about it or believed he needed to say more on the topic or had come to think he had not handled it properly, at least not treated it with the care it warrants.

It is not easily determined when and why Wittgenstein revisited the topic of colour and composed the remarks published in *Remarks on Colour*. No question that the material is drawn from three manuscript volumes that he compiled in the last fifteen months or so of his life. (Part I comprises 88 remarks drawn from MS 176, Part II 20 remarks drawn from MS 172, and Part III 350 remarks drawn from MS 173.) The drawback is that only the first 130 remarks of Part III are dated as having been written between 24 March and 12 April 1950. (III.1 is preceded by '24.3.50', III.127–130 by '12.4'.) In her Preface Anscombe notes that 'it is not clear whether Part II ante- or post-dates Part III' and states that 'Part I was written in Cambridge in March 1951'. This get the order of the three parts right but there is reason to think that Part II was written before Part III, most probably when Wittgenstein was in Vienna visiting his family between December 1949 and March 1950, and Part I was written earlier than Anscombe suggests. Part I is indeed 'a selection and revision of [Part III], with few additions', some two thirds of its remarks being recycled from Part III (with small changes), but it was in all probability compiled in the autumn of 1950, many months before Wittgenstein drafted his last remarks, remarks dated between 23 March and 27 April 1951 (OC §§426–676). (For further discussion see Lugg 2014a and 2021, Chapter Two.)

One thing of likely significance regarding Wittgenstein's interest in colour during the period is that in January 1950 he was reading Johann Wolfgang von Goethe's *Zur Farbenlehre* (*On the Theory of Colour*, published in 1810). In letters to Norman Malcolm, Georg Henrik von Wright and Rush Rhees, dated January 16, 19 and 22 respectively, he says he is finding Goethe's book 'philosophically interesting' if 'partly boring' (WC: 456–458). He does not, however, elaborate. He had previously read *Zur Farbenlehre* – in his letter to Rhees he speaks of rereading it – but nothing he had previously written about Goethe is plausibly regarded as shedding light on why he began to write on colour again. It is doubtful that he would have been moved to do so because he recalled 'Goethe's contempt for laboratory experiment' (CV: 20), the possibility that Goethe's 'passion for colour theory' was rooted in the fact that 'colours inspire philosophising' (MS 136: 92), the point that psychological theories of colour of the sort Goethe advanced are philosophically irrelevant (MS 155: 56v), or Goethe's injunction: 'Don't look for anything behind the phenomena' (*Remarks on the Philosophy of Psychology* I §889). But if none of this is plausibly taken to have rekindled his renewed interest in colour concepts, what in *Zur Farbenlehre* might he have found sufficiently 'philosophically interesting' to have sent him back to the drawing board?

In his 22 January letter to Rhees Wittgenstein says he has written 'some weak remarks', and it is plausibly conjectured that what inspired him to set down the remarks of *Remarks on Colour* is discoverable here if at all. (Wittgenstein's noting on 22 January 1950, when he wrote to Rhees, that he has set down some thoughts while reading *Zur Farbenlehre* is not, as has been suggested (WC:

458), in 'slight contradiction' with his saying on 16 January, when he wrote to Malcolm: 'I'm not writing at all because my thoughts never sufficiently crystallize'. They could have gelled, whatever they were, in the meantime.) The only difficulty is that none of the surviving manuscripts can be definitely pinned down to January 1950. The most probable candidate, however, is the first quarter of MS 172, subsequently published as Part II of *Remarks on Colour*. While MS 169, the sole other possible candidate, contains a number of important remarks on colour (LW II: 47–48), these were in all probability composed at the same time as remarks in MS 173, that is, after Wittgenstein had returned to England in March 1950. (MS 170 and MS 171 can be ruled out of contention, the only remark of any moment in either being a reminder about leaves changing from green to red being counted as reddish-green.) MS 172 is thus the sole remaining extant material in which colour figures significantly that fills the bill.

MS 172 itself comprises four loose sheets, one devoted to colour (reprinted as ROC II.1–20), the other three devoted to belief, doubt and other knowledge-related concepts (reprinted as OC §§1–65). (The fact that the manuscript consists of loose sheets also suggests the remarks were composed when Wittgenstein was away from his manuscript volumes and notebooks and making do with whatever writing material was at hand. Also it is worth noting in passing that Anscombe conjectures her 'Preface' for *On Certainty*, written almost a decade before the 'Editor's Preface' for *Remarks on Colour*, that Wittgenstein was in Vienna when he composed MS 172.) Since it is generally understood, though not universally accepted, that ROC II.1–10 was written before ROC II.11–20, it is a good bet that Wittgenstein showed his hand in ROC II.1–10, the first few remarks in particular. He begins, as he often does, with an uncontroversial general remark: 'We might speak of the colour-impression of a surface, by which we wouldn't mean the colour, but rather the composite of the shades of colour, which produces the impression (e.g.) of a brown surface' (ROC II.1). But the next four remarks are singularly illuminating as to why Wittgenstein revisited the topic of colour.

'Is that the basis of the proposition that there can be no clear transparent white?'

In the second remark of Part II of *Remarks on Colour* Wittgenstein introduces a problem that could well have spurred him to reconsider the logic of colour and go on to compose the remarks in Part III and Part I. He writes: 'Blending in white removes the *colouredness* from the colour; but blending in yellow does not – Is that the basis of the proposition that there can be no clear transparent white?' (ROC II.2). The question he is raising is why are there transparent yellow surfaces but no transparent white ones, and the answer he offers is that white differs from yellow inasmuch as it makes the surface less colourful, that is, paler. His thought is that the impossibility is traceable to the (grammatical) fact that whereas a yellow transparent surface becomes with the addition of yellow yellower (and no less transparent), with the addition of white it becomes whiter (and hence less transparent). This is puzzling and one may be forgiven for wondering whether it leaves us any the wiser regarding the impossibility of 'clear transparent white'. For the moment, however, the important thing to notice is that Wittgenstein has isolated a problem about colour he had not previously recognized. In 1929/1930 he had noticed that reddish blue but not reddish green is a possible colour and now he notices that transparent yellow but not transparent white are on a similar footing. (He could also have mentioned that there is transparent red, etc., but no transparent black.)

Could Wittgenstein have come across this problem in *Zur Farbenlehre*? Goethe does, to be sure, mention transparency a few times. He speaks of white as 'the simplest, brightest, first, opaque occupation of space', observes that 'transparency itself, empirically considered, is already the first degree of the opposite state', and refers to the 'tendency of a transparent medium to become only half-transparent' (*Theory of Colours*, #147, #148 and #238). These observations are, however, awfully obscure, and there is no indication that Wittgenstein noticed, let alone was struck by, them when rereading Goethe's book. Still, there is reason to believe Wittgenstein was alerted to the logical impossibility of white transparent surfaces by something in *Zur Farbenlehre*, the impossibility being expressly referred to in a letter from Philipp Otto Runge to Goethe included as an appendix to the text, a letter Wittgenstein certainly read. Runge is the most cited author in *Remarks on Colour* after Goethe, and Wittgenstein cannot have missed that Runge compares 'reddish green' with 'southwesterly northwind'. While he does not cite either remark in Part II of *Remarks on Colour*, in Part III he writes as from 'Runge to Goethe': 'Both white and black are opaque or solid . . . White water which is pure is as inconceivable as clear milk' (III.94; in Part I, at I.21, he cites the remark as from Runge).

In II.2 of *Remarks on Colour* Wittgenstein assumes without argument that 'transparent white' is as logically aberrant as 'reddish green', not merely empirically impossible. And at II.3 he adds: 'But what kind of a proposition is that, that blending in white removes the colouredness from the colour? As I mean it, it can't be a proposition of physics'. That is, he is implying, it is a proposition of logic, a grammatical proposition, there being for him, as already stressed, nothing between the purely factual and the purely conceptual, no proposition that has the a priori character of logic and the a posteriori character of science. As Wittgenstein immediately goes on to note: 'Here the temptation to believe in a phenomenology, something midway between science and logic, is very great', a temptation he clearly believed should be firmly resisted. It thus makes good sense that he should next ask, with an eye to clarifying the logic of the concepts of transparency and whiteness: 'What then is the essential nature of *cloudiness*? For red or yellow transparent things are not cloudy; white is cloudy' (II.4). The concept of cloudiness (and hence opacity) is, he is saying, logically connected to certain colours, notably white and black, but not others, notably yellow and red. Moreover he adds – in the form of a question (with a possible nod to Goethe) – that cloudiness conceals forms, something that obliterates light and shadow (II.5).

It is no good arguing that Wittgenstein is missing a trick, the impossibility of transparent white being contrary to the physical law that transparent surfaces transmit practically all incident light while white surfaces reflect or scatter most of it, and the logical point that no surface can both reflect and transmit incident light. Wittgenstein would think this explanation falls short since transparent white is logically impossible, not merely physically impossible because of how the world and the human visual system happen to be. The envisaged physical explanation gets things back to front, the physical impossibility of transparent white being entailed by its logical impossibility, not the other way around. What requires noting, Wittgenstein would insist, is not that transparent and white surfaces behave a certain way but that transparency and whiteness are mutually exclusive as a matter of logic. To explain the opacity (and lack of transparency) of white, what is required, he would contend, is a representation of transparency and whiteness comparable to the colour octahedron (or colour circle), that is, an account of the concepts and an explanation based on that account of the impossibility of the sort he offers in II.4–5. It is not by chance that he says (after a few incidental remarks about white, black and cloudiness): '"The blending in of white obliterates the difference between light and dark, light and shadow"; does that define the concepts more closely? Yes, I believe it does' (II.9).

To appreciate why Wittgenstein revisited colour in 1950, I am suggesting, the remarks of *Remarks on Colour* have to be read in the order written rather than, as more naturally, in the order published, that is, beginning with Part II rather than Part I. Transparent white is not mentioned before I.17, almost a quarter the way through Part I, and it is too easy to jump to the conclusion that one or more of the topics treated in I.1–16 – the nature of pure white, whether green is a primary colour, the possibility of a people who perceive reddish-green and the supposedly false assumption that it falls to psychology to account for normal vision – started the ball rolling. This is doubly unfortunate. Since there is no mention of transparent white in the remarks preceding I.17, Wittgenstein is apt to be regarded as revisiting one or more features of colours he had already examined (and as treating the impossibility of transparent white as something of an afterthought rather than as of primary interest). Also starting with Part I has the baneful effect of encouraging the thought that Wittgenstein means to discuss language-games involving colour rather than 'the logic of colour concepts'. In I.1, a remark recycled from the second half of Part III, Wittgenstein compares two sorts of language-game, and it is tempting to suppose he is no longer continuing along the lines of *Philosophical Remarks* and, arguably, even the *Tractatus*.

'The impression of a coloured transparent medium is that something is behind the medium'

Wittgenstein returns to the problem of explaining the impossibility of transparent white in Part III of *Remarks on Colour*, remarks drawn from MS 173. (MS 173 also contains a substantial series of remarks on 'the inner and the outer' reproduced in LW II: 61–71.) While not signalled in the text, Wittgenstein takes up other matters after writing III.1–130 and only later composed III.131–350, the last 55 remarks of which are also reproduced in LW II: 71–79. Since there is no indication of a break in the discussion, not even a line dividing III.131–350 from III.1–130, the fact that Wittgenstein returns to the topic of colour a third time is liable to go unnoticed. This is an important lapse if only because transparency and transparent white are discussed differently in the two halves of Part III, their being treated in III.1–130 as in Part II (with smallish additions and modifications), in III.131–350 in a significantly new way, indeed one that resulted in Wittgenstein revising his view of the logic of colour concepts fundamentally. It is not an unreasonable guess that this was an important, if not the sole, reason he took up the topic of colour yet again.

There are just a few remarks about transparency in III.1–130. At III.23 Wittgenstein observes that transparency is produced in paintings differently from opaqueness (a point already noted at II.13), and at III.24, he suggests that transparent white will be seen to be impossible if a transparent red is painted and white substituted for red, a point that prompts him to suggest that 'black and white ... have a hand in the business'. (Here again Wittgenstein is concerned with colour concepts, not paint.) Moreover at III.70 he states that 'both cloudiness and transparency can be painted', another, if tangential, reference to Part II, and at III.76 he adds, after noting that 'Runge says that there are transparent and opaque colours', that it would be wrong to think that different green paints are needed to paint green glass and green cloth. Finally at III.94 he quotes Runge on the logical incoherence of 'reddish green' and 'transparent white' and notes that

Runge says: 'If black merely made things dark, it could indeed be clear; but because it smirches things, it can't be'. Evidently Wittgenstein is still convinced that 'transparent white' is linguistically monstrous and thinks an explanation of how it differs from 'transparent red' is no less needed than an explanation of how 'reddish green' differs from 'reddish blue'.

When Wittgenstein turns his attention back to colour after discussing 'the inner and the outer', he first notes that empirical (temporal) and logical (non-temporal) propositions are categorically different, tenders some thoughts about white and pure red, and stresses that 'a *natural history* of colours would have to report on their occurrence, not on their *essence* [i.e. how they are as a matter of logical necessity]' (III.131-III.135). Then, having briefly introduced the subject, he offers another explanation of the impossibility of transparent white (III.136), the announcement of which may have been partly, if not wholly, what motivated him to examine colour yet again. He argues that were a black drawing on a white background seen through a transparent white surface, assuming such a surface were possible, the drawing would appear unchanged; that is, it would appear as if seen through a (colourless) transparent glass, not through a white (coloured) transparent glass. Evidently, he would have us agree there is no such colour as transparent white. While a transparent glass may seem white, it cannot be white (compare III.139–141 and III.146–149). The culprit is not the cloudiness of white but rather the nature of transparency. Constructing a "transparent white body"' is, Wittgenstein avers, 'like constructing a "regular biangle"' (compare III.138).

Despite providing a plausible explanation of why there is no such thing as transparent white at III.136ff, Wittgenstein is not done with the topic. '[If] the impression of a coloured transparent medium is that something is behind the medium', and transparent surfaces can be seen through, he writes at III.172, 'a thoroughly monochromatic visual image cannot be one of transparency'. Then, at III.173, perhaps worried that he is assuming that monochromaticity entails opacity (and non-transparency) rather than explaining it, he reprises the argument sketched at III.136. He notes that 'a black drawing on a white paper behind a transparent [white] medium must appear as though it were behind a colourless medium'. And at III.191, scouting yet another explanation, he writes: 'If a pane of green glass gives things behind it a green colour, . . . [a] white pane should . . . make everything whitish i.e. . . . *pale* . . . Even a yellow glass makes things darker, should a white glass make things darker too?' Here he is canvassing the thought that there is no such thing as a transparent white surface since objects seen behind such a surface, were one possible, would appear lighter (because white) and darker (because transparent), an obvious contradiction (also see III.179, III.185–186, III.192 and III.199–200).

Wittgenstein also rehearses similar arguments in remarks at the end of MS 169, a strong indication, surely, that they were written after the remarks of MS 172. (It is not a problem that MS 169 precedes MS 172 in von Wright's catalogue of Wittgenstein's papers or said in the 'Editors' Preface' of Volume 2 of *Last Writings* to have been composed in the fall of 1948 or spring of 1949. The remarks in question are set off by dividing lines, supressed in the published material, and may well have been jotted down at a later date.) In MS 169 itself Wittgenstein again presumes that black seen through a transparent white glass would appear black and white white 'just as through a colourless glass' and adds – this is new – that given that dark red would appear blackish pink, 'black probably will not remain black' (LWII: 47). Moreover he asks: 'Should yellow [seen through white] become whitish-yellow or white?' and responds that 'in the first case the "white" glass acts like colourless glass, in the second like opaque glass' (LWII: 48). This argument is of a piece with the remarks on transparent white in III.131–350 and altogether different from those in Part II and III.1–130. The focus is now on how objects would appear through transparent glass rather than on the cloudiness of white.

'Transparency and reflection only exist in the dimension of depth'

In the second half of Part III of *Remarks of Colour*, Wittgenstein supplements what he says at III.138 and III.172 about transparency and transparent white with numerous other remarks on the topic. He points out for the first time that transparency is logically related to behindness, it being characteristic of transparent surfaces that they possess 'see-through-ness' and objects be perceivable through them. Indeed he draws attention to the fact that there is 'a connection between three-dimensionality [and] light and shadow' (III.144), adds that '"transparent" could be compared with "reflecting"' (III. 148) and declares that 'transparency and reflection only exist in the dimension of depth of a visual image' (III.150). In addition he notes that when 'transparent' is applied to surfaces, 'it is not immediately clear which transparent glass we should say had the "same colour" as a piece of green paper' (III.181; also II.13 and III.23). And just as significantly, if not more so, he adds that the concept of transparency 'stands in unlike relations to the various colour concepts' since, unlike the concepts of white, red, green, etc., it cannot be explained 'by pointing to coloured pieces of paper' (III.189). (For more on Wittgenstein on transparency in Part III see Lugg 2021.)

Wittgenstein realizes he is easily, even naturally, read as providing a scientific account of transparency and offering scientific reasons why there are no transparent white surfaces, an impression he is at pains to skittle. He writes:

'Something white behind a coloured transparent medium appears in the colour of the medium, something black appears black [is] not a proposition of physics' (III.173) and, further assuring the reader, he notes that even when speaking 'in physical terms', 'we are not directly concerned with the laws of physics' (III.175; also III.180 and III.252). What concerns him is logic, not physics (or any other science). As he also says: 'We do not want to find a theory of colour (neither a physiological nor a psychological one), but rather the logic of colour concepts', in the present instance the logic of the concept of transparency (III.188). Nor is it fortuitous that at III.173 he states that the proposition about how white and black appear through a coloured medium is 'a rule of the spatial interpretation of visual experience' and at III.200 states that a similar proposition is 'a rule of the appearance of transparency'. For him rules fall in the province of logic (or grammar) and the propositions under discussion are no more statements of empirical fact than the proposition that anyone over two metres tall is over one metre tall.

In the early 1930s Wittgenstein took the colour octahedron to represent the logic of colour concepts perspicuously, and he now realizes it falls short because it fails to cover transparency, never mind provides the beginning of an explanation of the grammatical incoherence of 'transparent white'. The octahedron representation must, he recognizes, be augmented with a rule to the effect that white behind a coloured transparent surface appears the colour of the surface and black black. This fact – that transparency is logically linked to behindness and see-through-ness – is no small matter. (Compare III.142: 'The various "colours" do not all have the same connexion with three-dimensional vision'. Also note that 'transparent' connotes 'appearing across or through' and the German '*durchsichtig*' literally means 'through-seeable'.) It augurs a major shift in how the logic (or grammar) of colour needs to be understood. Prior to 1950 Wittgenstein assumed colour and space are separate departments of language, each perspicuously representable independently of the other. Now, in 1950, he recognizes that these departments are related. Space and colour are interdependent, and the grammars of colour concepts and spatial concepts interwoven.

An important additional point is that Wittgenstein does not purport in Part III to settle once and for all how the logic of transparency is to be understood and why it is that transparent white is a logically impossible colour. Rather the opposite, he presents and explores reasons for thinking that more needs to be said. After stating at III.172–173 that a white surface behaves like a green surface, he asks: 'Does the analogy [of a white glass] with the glass of other colours break down at any point?' (III.175). 'Is it *because* [white and green are differently related to other colours] that for white there is nothing analogous to a transparent green glass?' (III.178). Moreover he wonders why, 'if green becomes whitish through [a white transparent surface]', grey does not 'become more whitish, and … black … become grey' (III.193) and why it is not 'possible for a glass to leave white, black and grey unchanged and make the rest of colours whitish' (III.205). Also at III.208 he poses the question: 'Why do I feel a white glass must colour black [despite accepting] yellow is swallowed up by black?' At III.238 he finds it puzzling that 'green [is] drowned in the black, while white isn't'. And at III.252 he writes: 'The question is: 'What must the visual image be like … for it to appear to us as coloured and transparent?'

If nothing else, the discussion of transparency and transparent white in *Remarks on Colour* scotches a number of popular views of the sort of philosopher Wittgenstein was and what he was about, not least the widespread view that he dismissed philosophical problems out of hand. He regards it as uncontroversial that nothing can be both transparent and white and bends his energies to exploring the fact. (Compare Gaskin and Jackson 1951: 77: 'It would be fair to say that [in his classes Wittgenstein] tried to work his way into and through a question in the natural order and in the nontechnical way in which any completely sincere man thinking to himself would come at it'.) He comes at the problem in various ways, traces consequences of embracing different suggestions and seeks out difficulties that the problem and his solution spawn. He does not take the easy way out and appeal to what science tells is or what we normally say, still less throw away 'his talent and debas[e] himself before common sense' (Russell 1959: 159). Nor does he embrace philosophical therapy as widely understood as an alternative to philosophical theory. He spells out 'the logic of colour concepts', something that, he reckons, 'accomplishes that which is often unjustly expected from a theory' (III.188).

Other Discussions and Further Reading

Remarks on Colour has received relatively little attention, definitely much less, than *On Certainty*. But see McGinn 1991, Lee 1999, Brenner 1999: Chapter 4 ('Color and Number') and Lugg 2021. Its origins are discussed in more detail in Lugg 2014a and 2021: Chapter Two. For the dating of the remarks see von Wright (1993: 509), Nedo (1993: 46–47) and Lugg 2021: 20–22 (for Part II), 37 (for Part III) and 154–155 (for Part I). Salles (2001: 175–176) conjectures that the second half of Part II of *Remarks on Colour* (II.11–20) was written before the first half (II.1–10) and suggests MS 169: 77–80 (LW II: 47–48) is best regarded as Part IV of *Remarks on Colour*, that is, treated – as here – as subsequent to or contemporaneous with Part III. Both the conjecture and the suggestion are implemented in his Portuguese translation of *Remarks on Colour* (2009). Lee notes that Part II 'records the discovery of the problem about transparent white' (1999: 217) but does not mention that Wittgenstein associates its impossibility with the 'dimension of depth'. Westphal (1987: 19) argues that transparent white is impossible since transparent surfaces transmit practically all incident light while white surfaces reflect or scatter most of it. To account for the logical, as opposed to the physical, impossibility he invokes the notion of 'a real definition', one that unveils 'a real essence', a move abhorrent to Wittgenstein. For criticism see Horner (2000) and Lugg 2014b and 2017b as well as Lugg 2021: 184.

6 Wittgenstein on Colour, 1950: Additional Observations

'There is merely an inability to bring the concepts into some kind of order'

In the second half of Part II of *Remarks on Colour*, Wittgenstein briefly examines a variety of colour concepts other than transparent white (arguably another indication that II.11–20 was written after II.1–10). Transparent white is not entirely forgotten, the burden of II.13 being that while a red-tinted glass could be painted by laying down 'a great many gradations of red and of other colours adjacent to one another', there is no saying how a painting of a glass would appear were 'the places [to] become whitish where, before, [they were] bluish or reddish'. (Presumably we are expected to think the resulting glass would no longer be transparent.) For the most part, however, II.11–20 concern light and its effects and, more importantly, touch on how Wittgenstein sees philosophy and what he takes the 'analysis of concepts' to involve (II.16). Already at II.9 he spoke of himself as 'defin[ing] the concepts more closely' and at II.10 observed that were someone not to find the concepts more closely defined, 'it wouldn't be that he had experienced the contrary, but rather that we wouldn't understand him'. Now he discusses the logic of colour concepts more generally and deeply and states how he construes philosophical problems and how they should be handled.

After declaring at II.9–10 that he is concerned with clarifying concepts, at II.11 Wittgenstein says: 'In philosophy we must always ask: "How must we look at this problem in order for it to become solvable [*lösbar*]?"' This does not conflict with his contention in the *Investigations* that philosophical problems should '*completely* disappear' (PI §133). Wittgenstein is not reversing himself and conceding that, as philosophers of old would have it, many, if not all, philosophical problems are solvable. Leaving aside the fact that *lösbar* may be rendered as 'soluble', II.2–8 shows that he still regards philosophical problems as dissolvable. In these seven remarks he takes the conundrum of why transparent white is impossible to be resolved by clarifying the nature of transparency (and showing transparent white is logically different from transparent red). His thought is that solving the philosophical problem goes hand in hand with dissolving it. (Compare BT: 310: 'Problems are solved in the literal sense of the word – dissolved like a lump of sugar in water'.) The only change from what Wittgenstein earlier stated is that he now recognizes that there is much more to the logic of colour concepts.

How Wittgenstein understands problem-solving in philosophy is clarified in II.12, where he notes that in the case of a topic like colour 'there is merely an inability [*Unfähigkeit*] to bring the concepts into some kind of order'. Philosophical problems are, he intimates, bothersome for the simple reason the concepts involved in their statement are insufficiently well understood. We do not know how to proceed, do not have the relevant concepts properly organized. (Compare PI §123: 'A philosophical problem has the form: "I don't know my way about [*Ich kenne mich nicht aus*]"'.) When confronted by a philosophical problem, he adds (switching to the first-person plural): 'We stand there like the ox in front of the barn door'. (*Dastehen wie der Ochs vorm Scheunentor* is a common German idiom meaning 'to be stumped'.) Like the proverbial ox we cannot decide whether to go on, stay put or turn back, and we are obliged to engage in investigation of the sort Wittgenstein undertakes in II.2–8 and endeavour to bring the relevant concepts into 'some kind of order'. In particular, to avoid the dilemma in the case of transparent white, we need to recognize that whiteness is linked to cloudiness or note, as Wittgenstein later says, that transparency is linked to 'see-through-ness' and 'behindness'.

Wittgenstein explains his philosophical approach further when he writes: 'Phenomenological analysis (as, e.g., Goethe would have it) is analysis of concepts and can neither agree with nor contradict physics' (II.16). He is not suggesting that Goethe himself offers what is usually taken to be a 'phenomenological analysis', let alone an 'analysis of concepts'. Wittgenstein was as aware as anyone that Goethe believed Newton's theory of colour untenable and aimed to provide an alternative scientific theory. Nor is his remark at variance with his earlier taking phenomenology to be 'something midway between science and logic' (II.3). Whereas at II.3 he regards it as purporting to yield substantial truths about the world, at II.16 he takes it to be concerned with conceptual truths about language. His thought is that statements of interest to phenomenologists – 'Blending in white removes the colouredness from the colour' would be an example – are shown true by an 'analysis of concepts', not by intuition or other similar natural or non-natural means. He is again underlining that whiteness is connected with cloudiness as a matter of grammar, not fact (also compare NB: 106, PR: 273, and BT: 329).

In the balance of Part II of *Remarks on Colour* Wittgenstein briefly comments on a number of other logical features of colour. At II.14 he wonders whether the difference between painting a white glass and painting a transparent red glass is that 'colours remain saturated . . . when a reddish light is cast on them, while they don't with [a] whitish light'. (Presumably Wittgenstein is not forgetting that 'we don't speak of a "whitish light cast on things" at all'.) At II.15 he observes that were everything to look whitish in a particular light, we would not conclude 'the light source must look white', and at II.17 he asks – the English translation is missing a question mark – what we would say if 'the light of a white-hot body makes things appear light but whitish, and so weakly coloured; the light of a red-hot body makes thing appear reddish, etc'. Moreover at II.18 he questions whether it could happen that things appear in their full colours only 'in black light' and at II.19 adds: 'But wouldn't there be a contradiction here?' Finally at II.20 he writes: 'I don't *see* that the colours of bodies reflect light into [one's] eye.' These remarks are hardly perspicuous and might be among the 'weak remarks' that Wittgenstein refers to in his 22 January 1950 letter to Rush Rhees. (I take a stab at further clarifying them in Lugg 2021: 32–36.)

'The logic of the concept of colour is just much more complicated than it might seem'

Granting that Wittgenstein started writing Part III relatively soon after Part II, he is most naturally regarded as supposing he needed to re-examine the phenomenon of colour (and its logic) from scratch. Having realized he had failed in earlier writing to consider transparency and the impossibility of transparent white, he would doubtless have felt he ought to subject features of colour he had already discussed to more extensive scrutiny and check that his treatment of them passes muster. The blurb on the cover of the paperback edition of the book, probably approved, if not written, by G.E.M. Anscombe, is thus partly right, partly wrong. Wittgenstein discusses 'the features of different colours, of different kinds of colour (metallic colours, the colours of flames, etc.) and of luminosity' (compare III.106: 'The logic of the concept of colour is just much more complicated than it might seem'). But it is a stretch to describe this as his 'principal theme', one he treats 'in such a way as to destroy the traditional idea that colour is a simple and logically uniform kind of thing'. There are many other equally important themes and there is precious little in *Remarks on Colour* on the simplicity and logical unity of colour.

In Part III of *Remarks on Colour* Wittgenstein devotes considerable attention to the complexity and variety of concepts he had discussed in the 1930s and 1940s (as well as topics in addition to transparency discussed in Part II). Thus at

III.1 he revisits various concepts he had discussed in the 1930s and 1940s as well as the topic of coloured lights discussed in Part II. At III.1 he says (preceded by a question mark): 'White must be the lightest colour in a picture'. (This is partially retracted at III.57: 'It is not correct to say that in a *picture* white must always be the lightest colour', only 'it must be the lightest one in a flat pattern of coloured patches'.) And at III.70 he says: 'It is not true that a darker colour is at the same time a more blackish one. ... A saturated yellow is darker, but not more blackish than a whitish yellow'. (Also compare III.104: '"Dark" and "blackish" are not the same concept', and III.156: 'Black seems to make a colour cloudy, but darkness doesn't. ... Black is a surface colour. Darkness is not called a colour'.) In addition he considers pure (saturated) colours (III.4–21 and III.133–134), the difference between primary colours, which are listable, and saturated colours, which are not (III.25 and III.161), the claim that green is a primary as opposed to a mixture of blue and yellow (III.26 and III.158), the fact that 'a weak white light is not a grey light (III.218) and the point that 'we speak of a "dark red light", but not of a "black-red light"' (III.227).

On the theme of different kinds of colour, Wittgenstein also mentions the colours of gemstones, hair colour and the colours of metals and flames. At III.51 he notes that metallic colours like gold and silver are different from non-metallic colours like yellow and white, and at III.79 (and III.100) he notes that 'gold' is different from 'golden', inasmuch as it applies to metals as opposed to surfaces that have the appearance of gold (compare too III.258 on 'the colours of polished silver, nickel, chrome, etc'). Furthermore at III.70 he observes that amber is not blackish yellow and at III.151 observes that you would not call amber in a picture a monochromatic element of the surface. (Also at III.70 and later at III.156 and III.272, harking back to his discussion of cloudiness in Part II, he points out that he 'would not say of a ruby that it is blackish red, for that would suggest cloudiness'.) In addition at III.117 he underscores that 'blond' applied to hair colour is different from 'white' just as 'zinc coloured' applied to metal is different from 'grey' (also compare III.271–277). Finally at III.145 he states that the colour of a flame is not 'the property of a – visual – surface', at III.223 states it 'mean[s] nothing' to say 'a substance burns with a grey flame', and at III.240 notes that 'the peculiarity of white, grey and black would show up more clearly' were children taught 'the colour concepts by pointing to coloured flames'.

Wittgenstein also discusses in some detail 'luminous' and 'luminosity', neither of which he had previously considered. At III.57 he observes that 'a luminous yellow' may be lighter than a 'white paper in shadow' and at III.58 (and III.266) challenges the idea that the concept of a luminous point is more fundamental than the concept of a surface colour. (This suggestion, for all its initial plausibility, labours under the difficulty that points appear differently coloured in different surroundings.) Also at III.66 Wittgenstein observes that 'luminous' (along with 'iridescent', 'shimmering', 'glittering' and 'gleaming') applies to 'an extended area or . . . small expanses in a particular surrounding' and at III.156 stresses that 'luminous red' does not mean '*light* red', some dark reds being luminous too. Furthermore, returning to the topic, he notes at III.225 that a body might be seen '*now* as weakly luminous, *now* as grey', and states at III.228 that 'there is such a thing as the *impression* of luminosity'. Then, lastly, he points out at III.244–245 that 'luminous white' appears grey or 'weakly illuminated' white, 'for if I *paint* [luminous white] I may have to mix [grey] on the palette', the appearance of things again depending on how their neighbours are illuminated.

In the Preface to *Philosophical Investigations* Wittgenstein speaks of himself as being compelled by the nature of his investigation 'to travel over a wide field of thought criss-cross in every direction' (ix) and in Part III of *Remarks on Colour* (and to a lesser extent Part II) he likewise provides 'as it were, a number of sketches of landscapes'. Besides discussing pure colour, primaries, and various other colour concepts, he discusses the possibility of our communicating with a small number of colour words (ROC III.52), the fact that people have no idea or a false one of the meaning of most colour words (III.103), the way in which events appear in black and white films (III.185), and the difference between what he does and what gestalt psychologists do (III.221). Also, commenting on the structure of colour, he declares that the relations of lightness and darkness form 'a sort of mathematics of colour' (III.3) and writes: 'Among the colours: Kinship and Contrast. (And that is logic)' (III.46; also see III.12). (III.295–350, the remarks reprinted in Volume 2 of *Last Writing*, have more to do with 'the philosophy of psychology' than 'the logic of colour concepts' and may have been included in *Remarks on Colour* because the last three remarks of Part I are drawn from III.328–338.)

'The geometry of colours . . . shows us . . . that we are talking about colours'

The problem of accounting for the impossibility of 'forbidden colours' is not ignored in Part III of *Remarks on Colour*, just less prominent. In the *Tractatus* Wittgenstein holds that the joint occurrence of two colours is excluded by the logical structure of colour, in *Philosophical Remarks* holds that reddish green, bluish yellow, etc., are similarly excluded, and in Part II of *Remarks on Colour* holds that the same goes for transparent white (and transparent black). Now in Part III he turns the spotlight on the concepts of pure brown and luminous grey, both of which he takes to be equally linguistically aberrant, as well as saying more about reddish green and bluish yellow. As always, he presumes such impossibility is, since logical, grammatical. He gives the coldest of shoulders to the view that these colours are at most contrary to physical law and sidesteps arguments to the effect that they are inconceivable since physically, not logically, excluded. He does, however, worry that there could be a people with a system of colour terms relevantly similar to ours who can perceive reddish green and bluish yellow, all the while remaining convinced that the colour octahedron (and colour circle), understood as grammar, excludes them.

At III.60 Wittgenstein asks: 'Why don't we speak of "pure" brown?' and wonders whether this has to do 'merely' with its 'position ... with respect to the other "pure" colours'. In reply he notes that 'brown is, above all, a surface colour, i.e. there is no such thing as clear brown, but only a muddy one'. Moreover he states – hesitantly (there is a question mark in the text) – that brown contains black, and raises the question: 'How would a person have to behave for us to say of him that he knows a *pure, primary* brown'. Presumably Wittgenstein is entertaining the thought that there can be no pure brown since brown is a muddy colour, something pure colours never are. He is not, however, fully convinced, black-free browns being, he may well be thinking, a logical possibility. This is not an unreasonable response. Some bottles are clear brown just as some are clear green. Here, Wittgenstein notes, 'we must always bear in mind the question: How do people learn the meaning of colour names?', his thought being, I take it, that when one learns the use of 'brown', one learns that it applies to impure colours (III.62). In any event he goes on to say: 'What does "Brown contains black" mean? There are more and less blackish browns. Is there one which isn't black at all?' (III.62). To which he replies (the editor says he may have inserted a question mark): 'There certainly isn't one that isn't *yellowish* at all'. (In this connection it is worth remembering that browns are sometimes said to be dark yellows.)

Wittgenstein is less hesitant about the concept of luminous grey. He skirts the commonly held view that the casings of watches, gunmetal wheel rims and grey winter skies with the sun behind them are luminous grey and declares: 'There is no such thing as luminous grey' (ROC III.81). But rather than state straight-out that the colour is logically excluded, he asks: 'Is that part of the concept of grey, or part of the psychology, i.e. the natural history, of grey', and somewhat surprisingly adds: 'Isn't it odd that I don't know'. (Also compare III.156, where he says black 'takes away the luminosity of a colour' and asks whether that is 'something logical or something psychological'). Still later, however, he is less hesitant. He writes: 'That something which seems luminous grey cannot also appear grey ... teaches us something about our concept of white' (III.217) and wonders how it can be known merely from its appearance that the sky is not luminous, only illuminating (III.219). In addition he observes that things appear '"grey" or "white" only in a particular surrounding' (III 220) and states that, unlike Gestalt psychologists, he is asking: 'What is the impression of white, what is the meaning of this expression, what is the logic of this concept "white"?' (III.221).

While devoting some time to the logical impossibility of pure brown, luminous grey and transparent white, Wittgenstein accepts without argument, as he has done for decades, the logical impossibility of reddish green. Still he is bothered by the possibility of a people acquainted with the colour. He thinks it wrong to say 'they know other *colours*', there being 'no commonly accepted criterion for what is a colour, unless it is one of our colours', yet possible to 'imagine circumstances under which we would say, "These people see other colours in addition to ours"' (ROC III.42). It is, as he later puts it, both reasonable to suppose a people could have 'a geometry of colours different from our normal one' and reasonable to hold 'the geometry of colours shows what we're talking about' (III.86). (In III.87–88, not recycled in Part I, he notes 'the indefiniteness of the request to imagine [the colour]', and of knowing what we are supposed to consider as the analogue of something that is familiar to us'.) Might we not be in the position when it comes to perceiving reddish green comparable to the position the colour blind are in when it comes to distinguishing between red and green or the position those of us lacking perfect pitch are in comparable to those who possess it? From time to time Wittgenstein seems to toy with this possibility (see III.28–29, III.128–129 and III.292) but never takes it as decisive. (Evidently it is one thing to have a 'different talent' – see III.28 – another to perceive a different colour or sound.) Could it be, Wittgenstein asks – perhaps in despair – that his speaking of it being 'conceivable for our concepts to be different [was] all nonsense' (III.124)? But rather than accept that it was, he continues investigating the problem (see, for instance, III.163), albeit with seemingly no greater success.

In Part I of *Remarks on Colour* Wittgenstein restates the questions about impossible colours raised in Part III. He does not rework the earlier material but simply refines, reorganizes and cuts it down. The worries he had previously expressed are not allayed, questions are left hanging and residual conflicts are reproduced practically verbatim. Thus ROC III.42 and III.163 on reddish green are rewritten as I.14 and I.11 while III.150 and III.172–173 on transparent white are rewritten as I.19–20 and III.224–226 on luminous grey are rewritten as I.36–38. (By contrast, the chief remark on the impossibility of pure brown, III.60, is not recycled in Part I.) Wittgenstein does not rule out of court the possibility of a transparent white glass subsequent to deeming it a logically impossible colour (compare I.23–31). Nor does he dismiss the possibility of a people capable of perceiving reddish-green subsequent to deeming reddish-green logically impossible (compare I.77–82). To the end he remains dogged by the difficulty posed by suggestion that a people might perceive colours forbidden by our system of colour concepts. In the *Investigations* he says: '*Essence* is expressed in grammar. . .. Grammar tells what kind of object anything is' (PI §371 and PI §373). Here he is not so sure.

'We must always be prepared to learn something *totally* new'

When Part I of *Remarks on Colour* is read after Part III, there is a danger of it being regarded as adding nothing new and the book as a whole being decried as more 'repetitive than other posthumous works by Wittgenstein' (for this reaction and more on how the book has been received, see Lugg 2021: 172–174). Such criticism is misdirected. The collection of remarks is repetitive because Part I refines, reorganizes and condenses the remarks of Part III, and Wittgenstein repeatedly reconsiders problems he had not resolved to his own satisfaction. More than a few problems continued to eat away at him, and he was out to record what he had and had not figured out, what he refers to as results of his investigations (along with his more programmatic remarks). In particular he clearly wanted to put distance between his and Goethe's treatments of the problem of colour and should not be upbraided for repeating in Part I that Goethe took colours to result from the interaction of light and shadow at light-dark boundaries (ROC I.2 / III.132), noting other perceived failings of *Zur Farbenlehre* (I.56 / III.251) and stressing the similarity of Goethe's scientific theory to a schematic outline of sort William James provides in his psychology (I.70–72 / III.125–126).

Many thoughts expressed in Part III are restated word for word in Part I. In addition to discussing the impossibility of reddish-green, transparent white and luminous grey, Wittgenstein recycles remarks about lightness and darkness, primary colours, the concept of a pure colour, metallic colours and the colours of glowing bodies. For the reader who has worked through the 350 remarks of Part III, the main interest of the 88 remarks of Part I lies in how Wittgenstein reorganizes his discussion and what he decides to omit and to add. Judging from the fact that well over half of the remarks in Part I come from III.131–350, he seems to have believed what he wrote on returning to the subject a third time at III.131 best express what he was after. The two most significant exceptions, III.76 / I.17 and III.94 / I.21, cite Runge on transparent colours and the similarity of 'transparent white' to 'southwesterly northwind', doubtless an indication of the importance Wittgenstein accorded to the letter Goethe included as an appendix to *Zur Farbenlehre*. (Remarks added in Part I do not modify or supplement what he had earlier written. See, for instance, I.8–9 on intermediary colours and I.12–13 on colour blindness.)

What Wittgenstein says in *On Certainty* about norms of description could just as justifiably be said about the logic of colour concepts in *Remarks on Colour*. It also sounds 'all too reminiscent of the *Tractatus*' (OC, §321). In *Remarks on Colour*, as in the *Tractatus*, Wittgenstein intends his propositions to be understood as 'elucidatory' (TLP, 6.54), the object of the exercise being to represent colour concepts perspicuously with an eye to resolving philosophical puzzles about colour. The main difference is that in *Remarks on Colour* Wittgenstein recognizes that the logical structure of colour is far more complicated than he had assumed when writing the *Tractatus* (and appreciates that the colour octahedron at best represents relations among chromatic and achromatic primary colours. He still favours conceptual analysis though not as usually understood (or how it appears to figure in the *Tractatus*). For him the analysis of concepts is no longer regarded as explaining concepts in more fundamental terms but rather as clarifying them (so that philosophical problems occasioned by our language are obviated and philosophical mystery mongering forestalled). In his later thought, special cases aside, reductive analysis is superseded by the analysis of connections among concepts. (Compare PI §90: 'Substituting one form of expression for another … may be called "analysing" our forms of expression'.)

It is worth repeating, the point being regularly sloughed over, if not expressly denied, that Wittgenstein does not in later writings trade conceptual analysis for the study of language-games. When discussing colour he continues to examine the connections among concepts and to treat linguistic activity as concomitant. At no point in *Remarks on Colour* is colour language construed in terms of a human practice (or form of life) as opposed to something that can figure in such practice (or form of life). The phrase 'language-game' does not appear in Part II and plays no more than an incidental role in Part III and Part I. The purpose of the two language-games mentioned at III.131 / I.1 is to distinguish between internal and external relations among colour concepts and to highlight the difference between timeless and temporal propositions. Similarly the observation at III.158 / I.6 that 'there are language-games that decide [whether green should be counted as "a primary"]' does not entail that the meaning of 'primary' is keyed to practice, action or use. Nor does anything follow about meaning from I.8 on the existence of language-games for selecting 'intermediary or blended colours', the only other remark about language-games in Part I. (The same goes for the remarks in Part III not recycled in Part I. that mention language-games. Compare the suggestion at III.110 that one can become clear about 'the role of logic in colour concepts' by considering 'language-games in which, for example, things are put in a certain order'.)

While Wittgenstein does not resolve all the problems he tackles in *Remarks on Colour*, he achieves more than he normally receives credit for. The book is not, as has been suggested, a minor collection of remarks 'worth having as a late … work of a great mind' (Goodman 1978: 504). Nor is it merely 'one of the few documents that shows him concentratedly at work on a single philosophical issue', as important as this is (publisher's blurb). To the contrary, it provides a window into his approach to philosophy, early and late, and contributes more than a little to clarifying 'the problem of colour' and the ins and outs of colour language. Wittgenstein sets an agenda for philosophical work on colour and, arguably, works through it further than anyone else before or since. His question, 'What [do] I really want, to what extent [do] I want to deal with grammar' (ROC III.309), pretty much answers itself, this being a central concern, if not the central concern, of his remarks on the logic of colour concepts. As well as shedding light on what he could have been thinking when he said, 'One must not in philosophy attempt to short-circuit the problems' (AWL: 109), his remarks on colour crystalize what he meant when he opined: 'In every serious philosophical question uncertainty extends to the very roots of the problem. We must always be prepared to learn something *totally new*' (I.15 / III.44–45). (Also compare III.188, restated word-for-word at I.22: 'The logic of colour concepts … accomplishes that which people have often unjustly expected from a theory'.)

Other Discussions and Further Reading

See Ertz (2022: 115–116 and 247–249) for a brief overview of *Remarks of Colour*, and Lugg 2021 for a comprehensive treatment, pretty much remark by remark, of the whole volume. In connection with Wittgenstein's statement of how he views philosophy at ROC II.11–12, see the account of his approach in my (2000) and (2021). McGinn (1991: 442) takes Wittgenstein to believe we 'overestimat[e] … the degree of independence of colour concepts and spatial concepts' but sees him as mainly endeavouring to get clear in *Remarks on Colour* about 'two distinct but related language games', one 'for describing the colours of the natural world', the other associated with 'the precise system of colours that is defined by monochromatic samples of colour arranged on the colour wheel'. Hardin (1988: 124) holds in opposition to Wittgenstein that we do not perceive reddish green since the visual system comprises a red/green channel, a blue/yellow channel and a black/white channel and perception of one colour of each pair precludes perception of its companion.

References

Works by Wittgenstein Cited by Abbreviation

AWL   *Wittgenstein's Lectures: Cambridge 1932–1935*. Oxford: Blackwell, 1979.

BBB   *The Blue and Brown Books*, 2nd edition. Oxford: Blackwell, 1960 [1958].

BEE   *Nachlass: Bergen Electronic Edition*. Oxford: Oxford University Press, 2000.

BT   *The Big Typescript: TS 213*. Oxford: Blackwell, 2005.

CV   *Culture and Value*, revised edition. Oxford: Blackwell, 1998.

LFM   *Wittgenstein's Lectures on the Foundations of Mathematics: Cambridge 1939*. Chicago: University of Chicago Press, 1976.

LW   *Last Writings on the Philosophy of Psychology*, Volume I and II. Oxford: Blackwell, 1982.

LWL   *Wittgenstein's Lectures: Cambridge 1930–1932*. Oxford: Blackwell, 1980.

MWL   *Wittgenstein's Lectures: Cambridge 1930–1933*. Cambridge: Cambridge University Press, 2016.

NB   *Notebooks 1914–1916*, 2nd edition. Oxford: Blackwell, 1979 [1961].

OC   *On Certainty*. Oxford: Blackwell, 1969.

PI   *Philosophical Investigations*, 4th edition. Oxford: Blackwell, 2009 [1953].

PPF   *Philosophy of Psychology – A Fragment*. Oxford: Blackwell, 2009 [1953].

PR   *Philosophical Remarks*. Oxford: Blackwell, 1975.

PU   *Philosophische Untersuchungen*. Kritisch-genetische Edition. Frankfurt am Main: Suhrkamp, 2001.

PT   *Prototractatus*. London: Routledge, 1971 [1917].

RFM   *Remarks on the Foundations of Mathematics*, 2nd edition, Cambridge: MIT Press, 1978.

RLF   'Some Remarks on Logical Form'. In *Ludwig Wittgenstein: Philosophical Occasions 1912–1951*. Indianapolis: Hackett, 1993 [1929].

ROC   *Remarks on Colour*. Oxford: Blackwell, 1977.

RPP   *Remarks on the Philosophy of Psychology*, Volumes I and II. Oxford: Blackwell, 1980.

TLP   *Tractatus Logico-Philosophicus*. Translated by C. K Ogden. London: Routledge, 1933 [1922].

WC   *Wittgenstein in Cambridge: Letters and Documents 1911–1951.*
        Oxford: Blackwell, 2008.

WVC   *Wittgenstein and the Vienna Circle.* Oxford: Blackwell, 1979.

WWT   'Discussions between Wittgenstein, Waddington, and Thouless: Summer
        1941'. In *Public and Private Occasions.* Lanham: Rowman & Littlefield,
        2003.

Z   *Zettel.* Oxford: Blackwell, 1967.

Other References

Black, M. (1964). *A Companion to Wittgenstein's 'Tractatus.* Ithaca: Cornell
University Press.

Blank, A. (2008). 'Wittgenstein on Colours and Logical Multiplicities, 1930–
1932'. *Dialogue*, 47, 311–329.

Brenner, W. H. (1999). *Wittgenstein's Philosophical Investigation.* Albany:
SUNY Press.

Child, W. (2011). *Wittgenstein.* London: Routledge.

Dehnel, P. (2023). *The Radial Method of the Middle Wittgenstein.* London:
Bloomsbury.

Dreben, B. and J. Floyd (1991). 'Tautology: How Not to Use a Word', *Synthese*,
87, 23–49.

Engelmann, M. (2013). *Wittgenstein's Philosophical Development.* London:
Palgrave.

Engelmann, M. (2017). 'What does a Phenomenological Language Do?' In
M. Silva (ed.), *Colours in the Development of Wittgenstein's Philosophy*
(pp. 95–125), London: Palgrave.

Engelmann, M. (2018). 'Phenomenology in Grammar: Explicitation, Verification-
ism, Arbitrariness, and the Vienna Circle'. In O. Kuusela, M. Ometita, &
T. Uçan (eds.), *Wittgenstein and Phenomenology* (pp. 22–46), London:
Routledge.

Engelmann, M. (2020). 'Wittgenstein's Philosophical Remarks: On TS 208 and
TS 209', *Philósophos*, 25, 183–213.

Ertz, T.-P. (2006). 'Farben' and 'Bemerkungen über die Farben'. In A. Weiberg
& S. Majetschak (eds.), *Wittgenstein Handbuch: Leben – Werk – Wirkung*
(pp. 243–249 & 115–116), Berlin: Metzler.

Figueiredo, F. F. (ed.) (2023). *Wittgenstein's Philosophy 1929.* London:
Routledge.

Floyd. J. (2022). 'Bemerkungen über die Grundlagen der Mathematik'. In
A. Weiberg & S. Majetschak (eds.), *Wittgenstein Handbuch: Leben –
Werk – Wirkung* (pp. 104–107), Berlin: Metzler.

Gaskin, D. A. T. and A. C. Jackson (1951). 'Ludwig Wittgenstein', *Australasian Journal of Philosophy*, 29, 73–80.

Gierlinger, F. A. & S. Riegelnik (eds.) (2014). *Wittgenstein on Colour*. Berlin: De Gruyter.

Goldfarb, W. (2018). 'Moore's Notes and Wittgenstein's Philosophy of Mathematics: The Case of Mathematical Induction'. In D. Stern (ed.), *Wittgenstein in the 1930s* (pp. 241–252), Cambridge: Cambridge University Press.

Goodman, N. (1978). 'Book Review', *Journal of Philosophy*, 75, 503–504.

Griffin, J. (1964). *Wittgenstein's Logical Atomism*. Oxford: Oxford University Press.

Hacker, P. M. S. (1986). *Insight and Illusion*. Revised edition. Oxford: Oxford University Press.

Hardin, C. (1988). *Colour for Philosophers*. Indianapolis: Hackett.

Hilmy, S. S. (1987). *The Later Wittgenstein*. Oxford: Blackwell.

Hintikka, M. and J. (1986). *Interpreting Wittgenstein*. Oxford: Blackwell.

Horner, E. (2000). 'There Cannot be a Transparent White', *Philosophical Investigations*, 23, 218–241.

Jacquette, D. (1988). *Wittgenstein's Thought in Transition*. West Lafayette: Purdue University Press.

Kenny, A. (1973). *Wittgenstein*. Harmondsworth: Penguin.

Klagge, J. C. (2022). *Tractatus in Context*. London: Routledge.

Kuusela, O. (2023). 'The Colour-Exclusion Problem and the Development of Wittgenstein' Philosophy of Logic'. In F. F. Figueiredo (ed.), *Wittgenstein's Philosophy in 1929* (pp. 61–79), London: Routledge.

Landini, G. (2007). *Wittgenstein's Apprenticeship with Russell*, Cambridge: Cambridge University Press.

Lee, A. (1999). 'Wittgenstein's *Remarks on Colour*', *Philosophical Investigations*, 22, 216–239.

Lugg, A. (2000). *Wittgenstein's Investigations 1–133*. London: Routledge.

Lugg, A. (2010). 'Wittgenstein on Reddish Green: Logic and Experience'. In A. Marques & N. Venturinha (eds.), *Wittgenstein on Forms of Life and the Nature of Experience* (pp. 155–181), Bern: Peter Lang.

Lugg, A. (2013). 'Wittgenstein in the mid-1930s: Calculi and Language-Games'. In N. Venturinha (ed.), *Wittgenstein's Philosophical Investigations: Studies in Its Genesis* (pp. 135–154), London: Routledge.

Lugg, A. (2014a). 'When and Why was *Remarks on Colour* Written – and Why Is It Important to Know?' In F. A. Gierlinger & S. Riegelnik (eds.), *Wittgenstein on Colour* (pp. 1–19), Berlin: De Gruyter.

Lugg, A. (2014b). 'Wittgenstein on Transparent White', *Wittgenstein-Studien*, 5, 207–226.

Lugg, A. (2015a). 'Russell and Wittgenstein on Incongruent Counterparts and Incompatible Colours', *Russell*, 35, 43–58.

Lugg, A. (2015b). 'Wittgenstein on Colour Exclusion: Not Fatally Mistaken', *Grazer Philosophische Studien*, 92, 1–21.

Lugg, A. (2017a). 'Incompatible Colours and the Development of Wittgenstein's Philosophy'. In M. Silva (ed.), *Colours in the development of Wittgenstein's Philosophy* (pp. 33–55), London: Palgrave.

Lugg, A. (2017b). 'Impossible Colours: Wittgenstein and the Naturalist's Challenge'. In M. Silva (ed.), *How Colours Matter to Philosophy* (pp. 107–121), Berlin: Springer.

Lugg, A. (2019). 'Wittgenstein and Scientific Representation', *Wittgenstein-Studien*, 10, 211–226.

Lugg, A. (2021). *Wittgenstein's Remarks on Colour*. London: Anthem.

Lugg, A. (2022). 'Wittgenstein and the Representation of Colour'. In F. S. Velasco, N. A. R. Maza & K. M. C. Almanza (eds.), *Perspectivas Wittgensteinianas: Lenguaje, significado y acción* (pp. 69–100), Bogotá: Tirant lo Blanch.

Maund, B. (2018). 'Color'. In E. N. Zalta (ed.), *Stanford Encyclopedia of Philosophy*. Stanford University. https://plato.stanford.edu/archives/sum2018/entries/color/.

McGinn, M. (1991). 'Wittgenstein's "Remarks on Colour"', *Philosophy*, 66, 435–453.

McGuinness, B. (2002). *Approaches to Wittgenstein*. London: Routledge.

Moore, G. E. (1993 [1954–1955]), 'Wittgenstein's Lectures in 1930–33'. In J. Klagge & A. Nordmann (eds.), *Ludwig Wittgenstein: Philosophical Occasions 1912–1951* (pp. 46–114). Indianapolis: Hackett.

Monk, R. (2014). 'The Temptations of Phenomenology: Wittgenstein, the Synthetic a Priori and the "Analytic a Posteriori"', *International Journal of Philosophical Studies*, 22, 312–340.

Moss, S. (2012). 'Solving the Color Incompatibility Problem', *Journal of Philosophical Logic*, 41, 841–851.

Mounce, H. O. (1981). *Wittgenstein's Tractatus: An Introduction*. Chicago: University of Chicago Press.

Nedo, M. (1993). *Weiner Ausgabe, Einführung*. Wien: Springer.

Paul, D. (2007). *Wittgenstein's Progress*. Bergen: Wittgenstein Archives.

Pichler, A. (2018), 'Wittgenstein on Understanding: Language, Calculus, and Practice'. In D. Stern (ed.), *Wittgenstein in the 1930s* (pp. 45–60), Cambridge: Cambridge University Press.

Pinsent, D. H. (1990). *A Portrait of Wittgenstein as a Young Man*. Oxford: Blackwell.

Preston, J. (2015). 'Logical Space and Phase Space'. In D. Moyal-Sharrock, V. Munz & Annalisa Coliva (eds.), *Mind, Language and Action* (pp. 35–44), Berlin: De Gruyter.

Preston, J. (2017). 'Wittgenstein, Hertz and Boltzmann'. In H.-J. Glock, & J. Hyman (eds.), *A companion to Wittgenstein* (pp. 110–124), Oxford: Blackwell.

Ramsey, F. P. (1923). 'Review of the *Tractatus*', *Mind*, 32: 465–478.

Ramsey, F. P. (1990 [1929]). 'Theories'. In D. H Mellor (ed.), *Philosophical Papers* (pp. 112–137), Cambridge: Cambridge University Press.

Rothhaupt, J. G. F. (1996). *Farbthemen in Wittgensteins Gesamtnachlaß*. Beltz: Athenäum.

Russell, B. (1917). *Mysticism and Logic*. London: Allen and Unwin.

Russell, B. (1937 [1903]). *Principles of Mathematics*. 2nd ed. London: Allen and Unwin.

Russell, B. (1993[1959]). *My Philosophical Development*. London: Routledge, 1993.

Ryle, G. (1967). 'Ludwig Wittgenstein'. In K. T. Fann (ed.), *Ludwig Wittgenstein: The Man and His Philosophy* (pp. 116–125), New York: Dell.

Salles, J.-C. (2001). 'On Remarks on Colour', *Papers of the 24th International Wittgenstein Symposium*, Kirchberg am Wechsel: ALWS.

Schlick, M. (1979 [1932]). 'Form and Content'. In M. Schlick, *Philosophical Papers*, Volume II. Dordrecht: Reidel.

Schulte, J. (2014). 'We Have a Colour System as We Have a Number System'. In F. A. Gierlinger & S. Riegelnik (eds.), *Wittgenstein on Colour* (pp. 21–32), Berlin: De Gruyter.

Schulte. J. (2016). 'Wittgenstein's Last Writings'. In S. Rinofner-Kreidl & H. A. Wiltschepp (eds.), *Analytic and Continental Philosophy: Methods and Perspectives* (pp. 63–78), Berlin: De Gruyter.

Silva, M. (ed.) (2017). *Colours in the Development of Wittgenstein's Philosophy*. London: Palgrave.

Soames, S. (2003). *Philosophical Analysis in the Twentieth Century*, Volume I. Princeton: Princeton University Press.

Stern, D. (2018). 'Wittgenstein and Moore on Grammar'. In D. Stern (ed.), *Wittgenstein in the 1930s* (pp. 27–44), Cambridge: Cambridge University Press.

Trächtler, J. (2022). 'Bemerkungen über die Philosophie der Psychologie' and 'Letzte Schriften über die Philosophie der Psychologie'. In A. Weiberg &

S. Majetschak (eds.), *Wittgenstein Handbuch: Leben – Werk – Wirkung* (pp. 108–112), Berlin: Metzler.

von Goethe, J. W. (1970 [1810]). *Zur Farbenlehre (On the Theory of Colour)*. Cambridge, MA: MIT Press, 1970.

von Wright, G. H. (1993). 'The Wittgenstein's Papers'. In J. Klagge & A. Nordmann (eds.), *Ludwig Wittgenstein: Philosophical Occasions 1912–1951* (pp. 480–515), Indianapolis: Hackett.

von Wright, G. H. (1996). 'On Colour. A Logico-Philosophical Phantasy'. In *Six Essays in Philosophical Logic* (pp. 9–16). Helsinki: Societas Philosophica Fennica.

Westphal, J. (1987). *Colour: Some Philosophical Problems from Wittgenstein*. Oxford: Blackwell.

Acknowledgements

I benefitted from the questions and comments about themes explored in this Element when I presented them at Universitat de València, Universidade Nova de Lisboa, University of Ottawa, Virginia Commonwealth University and University of East Anglia. Thanks also to Paul Forster for many useful comments and suggestions on an early draft, to Warren Ingber for helping me in no small way prepare the final draft for publication, to Gary Kemp for much needed encouragement, to David Stern for sterling editorial assistance, to two anonymous reviewers for valuable criticism and advice, and to Felinda Sharmal and the team at Integra Software Services for shepherding my text so expertly and thoughtfully through the press.

The Philosophy of Ludwig Wittgenstein

David G. Stern
University of Iowa

David G. Stern is a Professor of Philosophy and a Collegiate Fellow in the College of Liberal Arts and Sciences at the University of Iowa. His research interests include history of analytic philosophy, philosophy of language, philosophy of mind, and philosophy of science. He is the author of *Wittgenstein's Philosophical Investigations: An Introduction* (Cambridge University Press, 2004) and *Wittgenstein on Mind and Language* (Oxford University Press, 1995), as well as more than 50 journal articles and book chapters. He is the editor of *Wittgenstein in the 1930s: Between the 'Tractatus' and the 'Investigations'* (Cambridge University Press, 2018) and is also a co-editor of the *Cambridge Companion to Wittgenstein* (Cambridge University Press, 2nd edition, 2018), *Wittgenstein: Lectures, Cambridge 1930–1933, from the Notes of G. E. Moore* (Cambridge University Press, 2016) and *Wittgenstein Reads Weininger* (Cambridge University Press, 2004).

About the Series

This series provides concise and structured introductions to all the central topics in the philosophy of Ludwig Wittgenstein. The Elements are written by distinguished senior scholars and bright junior scholars with relevant expertise, producing balanced and comprehensive coverage of the full range of Wittgenstein's thought.

For EU product safety concerns, contact us at Calle de José Abascal, 56–1°,
28003 Madrid, Spain or eugpsr@cambridge.org.

www.ingramcontent.com/pod-product-compliance
Ingram Content Group UK Ltd.
Pitfield, Milton Keynes, MK11 3LW, UK
UKHW022222270525
458834UK00015B/95